The Ultimate WordPress & WooCommerce Handbook - From Setup to Success in Online Selling

Anelly Aya

Table of Contents

Chapter 1: Introduction to WordPress and WooCommerce: The Foundations of E-Commerce....3

Chapter 2: Why Choose WooCommerce? Advantages for Online Store Owners 8

Chapter 3: Setting Up Your WordPress Environment: Hosting, Domains, and Installation 14

Chapter 4: Navigating the WordPress Dashboard: Your Command Center....19

Chapter 5: Installing and Configuring WooCommerce: A Step-by-Step Guide 25

Chapter 6: Understanding WooCommerce Settings: Tailoring Your Store's Core Features....31

Chapter 7: Choosing the Perfect Theme for Your Store: Design That Converts 38

Chapter 8: Customizing Your WooCommerce Store: Plugins and Page Builders 44

Chapter 9: Adding Products: Simple, Variable, Digital, and More 50

Chapter 10: Crafting Effective Product Descriptions and Images....56

Chapter 11: Setting Up Payment Gateways: Secure and Seamless Transactions....62

Chapter 12: Configuring Shipping Options: Local, International, and Custom Rates 69

Chapter 13: Tax Settings Made Easy: Compliance Without Complexity....75

Chapter 14: Managing Inventory: Stock Levels, Alerts, and Automation 81

Chapter 15: Creating a User-Friendly Checkout Experience 87

Chapter 16: Marketing Essentials: Coupons, Discounts, and Upselling....92

Chapter 17: Leveraging SEO for WooCommerce: Driving Organic Traffic to Your Store 97

Chapter 18: Social Media Integration: Using Platforms to Boost Sales 102

Chapter 19: Email Marketing for WooCommerce: Building Relationships with Customers 107

Chapter 20: Understanding WooCommerce Analytics: Metrics That Matter 112

Chapter 21: Scaling Your Store: Adding New Products and Features 117

Chapter 22: Handling Customer Support: Tools and Best Practices....122

Chapter 23: Mobile Optimization: Making Your Store Accessible Everywhere 128
Chapter 24: WooCommerce Security: Protecting Your Store and Customers 134
Chapter 25: Troubleshooting Common WooCommerce Issues 140
Chapter 26: Case Studies of Successful WooCommerce Stores 146
Chapter 27: The Future of WooCommerce: Trends and Innovations 152

Chapter 1: Introduction to WordPress and WooCommerce: The Foundations of E-Commerce

In today's digital age, e-commerce has revolutionized how businesses operate. With online sales booming worldwide, entrepreneurs are increasingly turning to digital platforms to create and scale their online stores. Among the plethora of options available, WordPress and WooCommerce have emerged as leading tools for building and managing e-commerce websites. This chapter introduces the fundamentals of these platforms, providing you with the foundational knowledge necessary to embark on your e-commerce journey.

What is WordPress?

WordPress is a content management system (CMS) that powers over 40% of the websites on the internet. Initially launched in 2003 as a blogging platform, WordPress has evolved into a robust tool for creating all types of websites, from personal blogs to complex e-commerce sites.

Key features of WordPress include:

- **Flexibility:** You can create virtually any website, from a portfolio to an online store.
- **User-Friendly Interface:** WordPress offers an intuitive dashboard for managing content.
- **Extensibility:** With thousands of plugins and themes, you can customize your site to suit your needs.
- **Community Support:** The extensive WordPress community offers free resources, forums, and tutorials.

What is WooCommerce?

WooCommerce is a powerful plugin designed to transform WordPress into a fully functional e-commerce platform. Launched in 2011, it quickly gained popularity due to its ease of use and comprehensive features.

Key features of WooCommerce include:

- **Ease of Integration:** Seamlessly integrates with WordPress.
- **Customizability:** Offers endless options to design and enhance your online store.
- **Scalability:** Suitable for both small startups and large enterprises.
- **Affordability:** The core plugin is free, with paid extensions available for advanced functionality.

The Importance of WordPress and WooCommerce in E-Commerce

The e-commerce industry thrives on flexibility, affordability, and efficiency—qualities that WordPress and WooCommerce deliver in abundance. These platforms empower businesses to:

1. **Reach Global Audiences:** Build a store accessible to customers worldwide.

2. **Reduce Costs:** Save on development costs with their user-friendly interfaces and free features.
3. **Gain Control:** Maintain ownership of your site, unlike marketplace platforms like Amazon or Etsy.
4. **Adapt Quickly:** Implement changes and updates with minimal downtime.

Core Advantages of Using WordPress and WooCommerce Together

1. **Cost-Effectiveness**
   WordPress and WooCommerce are open-source platforms, making them budget-friendly for entrepreneurs. While premium themes, plugins, and hosting come with costs, they are often far lower than hiring developers for custom solutions.
2. **Endless Customization**
   With thousands of themes and plugins available, you can tailor your store's appearance and functionality to align with your brand.
3. **SEO-Friendly Design**
   WordPress and WooCommerce offer SEO tools to help your store rank higher in search engine results, ensuring greater visibility and organic traffic.
4. **Scalability**
   Whether you're starting with ten products or thousands, WooCommerce scales effortlessly, adapting to the size and demands of your business.
5. **Community Support and Resources**
   Both platforms have large communities of developers, designers, and users who share valuable insights and solutions.

Understanding the E-Commerce Landscape

Before delving into technicalities, it's crucial to understand the broader context of e-commerce:

- **Market Growth:** Global e-commerce sales surpassed $5 trillion in 2022, highlighting the massive potential for online stores.
- **Consumer Behavior:** Buyers increasingly prefer the convenience of online shopping, with mobile devices playing a significant role in transactions.
- **Competition:** Success requires standing out through excellent design, user experience, and marketing strategies.

Building Your Store: Why Start with WordPress and WooCommerce?

Starting your e-commerce journey with WordPress and WooCommerce is ideal for several reasons:

1. **Ease of Use for Beginners**
   With minimal technical knowledge, you can set up a professional-looking store. User-friendly interfaces and guided setups make the process seamless.
2. **Ownership and Control**
   Unlike hosted platforms like Shopify or Wix, WordPress ensures you own your store's data, design, and functionality.
3. **Integration with Other Tools**
   WooCommerce easily integrates with payment gateways, email marketing platforms, and analytics tools to provide a holistic e-commerce experience.
4. **Room to Experiment and Grow**
   As your business grows, you can add features like subscription models, advanced shipping options, or multi-language support.

Key Components of a WordPress and WooCommerce Store

1. **Themes**
   Themes dictate your store's design. Choose a responsive, WooCommerce-compatible theme to ensure your site looks great on all devices.
2. **Plugins**
   Plugins extend your store's functionality. Popular examples include SEO tools, payment processors, and customer support features.
3. **Products**
   WooCommerce allows you to sell physical, digital, and subscription-based products. Each type comes with tailored options for pricing, descriptions, and delivery.
4. **Checkout and Payment Systems**
   WooCommerce supports multiple payment gateways, including PayPal, Stripe, and bank transfers, ensuring secure and convenient transactions.
5. **Analytics and Reports**
   Built-in analytics tools help you track sales, customer behavior, and inventory, enabling data-driven decision-making.

Challenges and How to Overcome Them

While WordPress and WooCommerce are user-friendly, beginners may face challenges, such as:

1. **Choosing the Right Hosting Provider**
   Solution: Opt for reliable hosting providers like Bluehost, SiteGround, or WP Engine, which offer optimized performance for WordPress sites.
2. **Ensuring Security**
   Solution: Use SSL certificates, update plugins regularly, and install security plugins like Wordfence or Sucuri.

3. **Customizing Themes and Plugins**
   Solution: Start with free options and invest in premium versions as your store grows. Online tutorials and forums can help bridge knowledge gaps.

4. **Competing in a Crowded Market**
   Solution: Focus on niche markets, exceptional customer service, and effective marketing strategies.

Case Studies: Success with WordPress and WooCommerce

1. **Boutique Retailer Expansion**
   A small artisan jewelry brand used WordPress and WooCommerce to expand from local markets to international audiences, leveraging social media integration and email campaigns.

2. **Digital Product Store**
   A graphic designer built a WooCommerce store for selling digital templates, achieving scalability without significant upfront costs.

3. **Subscription-Based Business**
   A fitness trainer launched a subscription-based workout program using WooCommerce's recurring payments feature, creating a steady revenue stream.

Summary

WordPress and WooCommerce provide an accessible, affordable, and highly customizable platform for launching an online store. Together, they empower entrepreneurs to create professional, scalable e-commerce sites without the need for extensive technical expertise. By leveraging their flexibility and integrating tools like SEO and analytics, businesses can thrive in today's competitive digital marketplace.

Key Takeaways:

- WordPress and WooCommerce are ideal for beginners and experienced users alike, offering affordability and customization.
- The e-commerce landscape is vast and growing, presenting significant opportunities for businesses of all sizes.
- Understanding the components of a successful WooCommerce store—themes, plugins, and payment systems—is essential.
- Challenges can be overcome with proper planning, tools, and community support.

This foundational knowledge sets the stage for deeper exploration in subsequent chapters, where we'll dive into building, managing, and scaling your WooCommerce store.

Chapter 2: Why Choose WooCommerce? Advantages for Online Store Owners

When it comes to launching an online store, the platform you choose plays a critical role in determining your business's success. WooCommerce has become a leading e-commerce solution, powering over 6 million websites worldwide. This chapter explores why WooCommerce stands out among competitors, delving into its features, benefits, and the strategic advantages it offers to online store owners.

What is WooCommerce?

WooCommerce is a free, open-source WordPress plugin designed to transform any WordPress website into a fully functional online store. Launched in 2011 by WooThemes, WooCommerce quickly gained popularity for its simplicity, scalability, and flexibility.

Unlike proprietary e-commerce platforms like Shopify, WooCommerce gives users full control over their stores, enabling them to design, manage, and grow their businesses without the constraints of a closed ecosystem.

Core Advantages of WooCommerce

1. Cost-Effectiveness

WooCommerce is free to install and use, making it an ideal choice for businesses of all sizes, from small startups to large enterprises. While you may incur additional costs for premium themes, plugins, or hosting, the base functionality is accessible to everyone.

Key Points:

- **Free Core Features:** Essential features like product listings, shopping carts, and payment processing are included at no cost.
- **No Transaction Fees:** Unlike some platforms, WooCommerce doesn't charge transaction fees, allowing you to retain more profit.
- **Flexible Budgeting:** Pay only for the specific tools and extensions your business needs.

---

2. Seamless Integration with WordPress

Since WooCommerce is built on WordPress, it integrates seamlessly into the ecosystem, leveraging WordPress's powerful CMS capabilities. This synergy allows you to:

- **Combine Content and Commerce:** Create blogs, tutorials, or videos alongside your store to attract and retain customers.
- **Use Existing Themes and Plugins:** Extend your site's functionality using thousands of WordPress plugins and themes.

- **Benefit from WordPress Updates:** Regular updates to WordPress automatically enhance your WooCommerce store's performance and security.

---

3. Flexibility and Customization

WooCommerce's open-source nature allows for unlimited customization, empowering store owners to tailor every aspect of their store. Whether you want a minimalist design or a feature-rich store, WooCommerce has you covered.

Customization Highlights:

- **Themes:** Choose from a variety of free and premium themes, including WooCommerce-specific options like Storefront.
- **Plugins:** Add features such as subscription services, dynamic pricing, or customer rewards programs.
- **Code Modifications:** Developers can modify WooCommerce's code to create unique functionalities tailored to your business.

---

4. Scalability for Growth

One of WooCommerce's standout features is its ability to scale with your business. Whether you're selling 10 products or 10,000, WooCommerce grows with you, ensuring a smooth transition from startup to enterprise.

Scalability Features:

- **Add Unlimited Products:** There's no limit to the number of products you can add.
- **Handle High Traffic:** With proper hosting, WooCommerce can manage high traffic volumes without compromising performance.
- **Expand with Extensions:** Easily add new functionalities like international shipping or multi-currency support as your business grows.

---

5. Diverse Product Options

WooCommerce accommodates a variety of product types, giving you the flexibility to sell:

- **Physical Products:** Traditional items that require shipping.
- **Digital Products:** Software, eBooks, music, and more.
- **Services:** Book appointments, consultations, or workshops.
- **Subscriptions:** Create recurring revenue with subscription-based products.
- **Variable Products:** Offer multiple variations of a single product (e.g., sizes, colors).

This versatility allows store owners to adapt to changing market demands and explore new revenue streams.

---

6. Advanced SEO Capabilities

WooCommerce is designed to work seamlessly with WordPress, a platform renowned for its SEO friendliness. With WooCommerce, you can optimize your online store to rank higher in search engine results, attracting more organic traffic.

Key SEO Advantages:

- **SEO Plugins:** Use tools like Yoast SEO to optimize product pages and blog posts.
- **Custom URLs:** Create search-engine-friendly URLs for products and categories.
- **Mobile-Friendly Design:** WooCommerce sites are responsive, ensuring better rankings on mobile searches.
- **Rich Snippets:** Implement structured data to display product ratings, prices, and availability directly in search results.

---

7. Wide Range of Payment Gateways

WooCommerce supports a variety of payment options, ensuring convenience for customers and flexibility for store owners. Some of the most popular gateways include:

- **PayPal and Stripe:** Easy-to-setup global payment solutions.
- **Direct Bank Transfer:** Ideal for businesses that cater to local markets.
- **Cash on Delivery (COD):** Useful for customers who prefer offline payments.
- **Regional Gateways:** WooCommerce supports country-specific gateways, ensuring compatibility with local payment preferences.

Extensions are also available for more specialized payment needs, such as recurring billing or cryptocurrency.

---

8. Robust Analytics and Reporting

WooCommerce provides built-in analytics tools that help store owners make data-driven decisions. From tracking sales to monitoring customer behavior, the platform offers valuable insights to optimize your store's performance.

Key Metrics Include:

- Sales figures and revenue trends.
- Customer acquisition and retention rates.
- Product performance, including bestsellers and underperforming items.

- Inventory levels and stock alerts.

Advanced users can integrate third-party tools like Google Analytics or CRM systems for even deeper insights.

---

9. Strong Community and Support

WooCommerce's vast community of developers, designers, and users is a major asset. Whether you're troubleshooting an issue or looking for inspiration, the community offers extensive resources, including:

- **Forums and Blogs:** Official WooCommerce forums and third-party blogs provide solutions to common problems.
- **YouTube Tutorials:** Step-by-step guides on setup, customization, and troubleshooting.
- **Premium Support:** Access dedicated support services with WooCommerce's premium plans.

---

10. Security and Compliance

E-commerce security is paramount, and WooCommerce offers several tools and practices to protect your store and customers.

- **SSL Certificates:** Ensure secure transactions by encrypting data.
- **Regular Updates:** Frequent updates to WooCommerce and WordPress address security vulnerabilities.
- **Plugins for Security:** Tools like Wordfence and Sucuri add an extra layer of protection.
- **GDPR Compliance:** WooCommerce provides features to ensure compliance with data privacy regulations.

How WooCommerce Compares to Competitors

1. **WooCommerce vs. Shopify**

- **Cost:** Shopify has a monthly subscription fee, while WooCommerce is free (excluding hosting and extensions).
- **Customization:** WooCommerce allows unlimited customization, while Shopify has limitations.
- **Ownership:** WooCommerce offers complete ownership of your store, unlike Shopify, which controls your data.

2. **WooCommerce vs. Wix**

- **Scalability:** WooCommerce is better suited for large stores or those expecting rapid growth.
- **Extensions:** WooCommerce has a broader range of plugins for advanced functionality.
- **SEO:** WooCommerce offers superior SEO capabilities compared to Wix.

3. **WooCommerce vs. BigCommerce**

- **Ease of Use:** BigCommerce is easier for beginners, but WooCommerce offers more flexibility for experienced users.
- **Cost:** BigCommerce's pricing is higher, especially for large-volume sellers.
- **Integration:** WooCommerce integrates more seamlessly with WordPress for content management.

Case Studies: Real-World Success with WooCommerce

1. **The Handmade Craft Store**
   A small business selling handmade crafts launched a WooCommerce store, leveraging its affordability and flexibility to showcase unique products. Within a year, the store doubled its revenue by integrating WooCommerce's marketing and analytics tools.
2. **The International Clothing Brand**
   A mid-sized clothing retailer used WooCommerce to expand globally, utilizing multi-currency plugins and international shipping extensions. WooCommerce's scalability allowed the brand to handle seasonal spikes in traffic.
3. **The Subscription-Based Wellness Service**
   A wellness company introduced subscription-based products using WooCommerce's extensions. This recurring revenue model contributed to sustained growth and improved customer retention.

Summary

WooCommerce's robust features, affordability, and scalability make it a top choice for online store owners. By integrating seamlessly with WordPress, offering extensive customization options, and supporting diverse product types, WooCommerce empowers businesses to thrive in a competitive market.

Key Takeaways:

- **Cost-Effective:** The core plugin is free, with optional paid features.
- **Customizable:** Tailor every aspect of your store, from design to functionality.
- **Scalable:** Adapt your store as your business grows.
- **SEO-Friendly:** Enhance visibility with WooCommerce's advanced SEO tools.
- **Global Reach:** Support for multiple languages, currencies, and payment gateways.

As you proceed through this book, you'll learn how to harness these advantages, turning your e-commerce vision into a reality. In the next chapter, we'll explore the technical aspects of setting up your WordPress environment to prepare for WooCommerce integration.

Chapter 3: Setting Up Your WordPress Environment: Hosting, Domains, and Installation

A robust WordPress environment is the foundation of any successful WooCommerce store. Before diving into designing your website or adding products, you must establish the technical groundwork. This chapter will guide you through selecting the right hosting provider, registering a domain name, and installing WordPress. Each step is critical to creating a fast, secure, and reliable online store.

Understanding the Basics: Hosting, Domains, and WordPress

What is Hosting?

Web hosting is a service that stores your website's files and makes them accessible on the internet. Think of hosting as renting a space for your website on the web. For an e-commerce store, hosting quality directly impacts your site's performance, speed, and uptime.

What is a Domain Name?

A domain name is your website's address, like www.example.com. It is how customers find and access your store. Choosing a domain that is relevant, memorable, and aligns with your brand is crucial.

Why WordPress?

WordPress is a versatile content management system (CMS) that simplifies website creation. Combined with WooCommerce, WordPress becomes a powerful platform for e-commerce. Before setting up WooCommerce, you need a properly configured WordPress installation.

Step 1: Choosing the Right Hosting Provider

Key Factors to Consider

1. **Performance:** Fast loading times are critical for user experience and SEO. Choose a provider with high-speed servers.
2. **Uptime Guarantee:** Look for hosting with a minimum uptime guarantee of 99.9% to ensure your site is always accessible.
3. **Scalability:** As your business grows, your hosting should accommodate increased traffic and data needs.
4. **E-Commerce Features:** Ensure the provider offers tools like SSL certificates, backups, and compatibility with WooCommerce.
5. **Support:** Reliable 24/7 customer support is essential for troubleshooting technical issues.

Popular Hosting Providers for WordPress

1. **Bluehost:** Affordable plans, great for beginners, and recommended by WordPress.
2. **SiteGround:** Known for excellent performance, security, and support.

3. **WP Engine:** A premium option focused on speed, scalability, and managed WordPress hosting.
4. **DreamHost:** User-friendly and offers free SSL certificates and daily backups.
5. **Hostinger:** Budget-friendly with robust features for small businesses.

Hosting Types Explained

1. **Shared Hosting:** Multiple websites share the same server. Suitable for small stores but limited in scalability.
2. **VPS Hosting:** A virtual private server provides more resources and control, ideal for growing businesses.
3. **Dedicated Hosting:** A server exclusively for your site, offering maximum performance but at a higher cost.
4. **Managed WordPress Hosting:** Tailored for WordPress sites, with automatic updates and optimizations.

Step 2: Registering Your Domain Name

Tips for Choosing a Domain Name

1. **Keep it Simple:** Short, easy-to-spell domains are more memorable.
2. **Include Keywords:** Incorporate words relevant to your niche (e.g., EcoFashionStore.com for sustainable clothing).
3. **Use .com if Possible:** While other extensions like .shop or .store are growing in popularity, .com is still the most trusted.
4. **Avoid Numbers and Hyphens:** These can confuse visitors and reduce credibility.
5. **Check Availability:** Use tools like Namecheap or GoDaddy to see if your desired domain is available.

Where to Register a Domain Name

1. **Domain Registrars:** Platforms like Namecheap, GoDaddy, or Google Domains specialize in domain registration.
2. **Hosting Providers:** Many hosting companies (e.g., Bluehost) offer free domain registration for the first year as part of their plans.

Step 3: Installing WordPress

Once you have hosting and a domain, the next step is to install WordPress. Most hosting providers offer a streamlined installation process.

Installation Methods

1. **One-Click Installations**
   Most hosting providers include one-click WordPress installation tools. Examples include:

- cPanel (used by Bluehost, HostGator, and others).
- Custom dashboards like SiteGround's Site Tools.

Steps:

1. Log in to your hosting account.
2. Navigate to the WordPress Installer.
3. Enter your domain name, choose a username and password, and click "Install."
4. **Manual Installation**
   If your hosting provider doesn't offer a one-click installer, follow these steps:
5. Download WordPress from wordpress.org.
6. Upload the files to your server using FTP (e.g., FileZilla).
7. Create a database in your hosting account's control panel.
8. Run the WordPress installer by visiting your domain.
9. **Managed WordPress Hosting**
   Providers like WP Engine or Kinsta pre-install WordPress, eliminating the need for manual setup. Simply log in and start customizing your site.

Step 4: Configuring Your WordPress Installation

1. Set Up Your Admin Account

Choose a strong username and password for your WordPress admin account. Avoid default usernames like "admin" to enhance security.

2. Update Permalink Structure

Permalinks define how URLs are structured on your site. For e-commerce stores, a clean and SEO-friendly format is essential.

- Go to **Settings > Permalinks** and select "Post Name" or customize as needed.

3. Install an SSL Certificate

SSL certificates encrypt data transferred between your site and its visitors, ensuring secure transactions. Most hosting providers offer free SSL certificates through Let's Encrypt.

- Activate SSL via your hosting dashboard or WordPress settings.

4. Configure Basic Settings

- **Site Title and Tagline:** Set these under **Settings > General.**

- **Time Zone:** Adjust for your region to ensure accurate order timestamps.

5. Install Essential Plugins

Plugins enhance your site's functionality. Install these basics:

- **WooCommerce:** To set up your store.
- **Yoast SEO:** For search engine optimization.
- **UpdraftPlus:** For backups.
- **Wordfence Security:** For website protection.

Step 5: Testing Your Environment

Before proceeding to WooCommerce setup, ensure your WordPress installation is functioning correctly.

1. **Check Site Speed:** Use tools like Google PageSpeed Insights or GTmetrix to evaluate loading times.
2. **Test Responsiveness:** Verify that your site is mobile-friendly by resizing your browser window or using Google's Mobile-Friendly Test.
3. **Verify SSL Installation:** Confirm the padlock icon appears in the browser's address bar.

Common Issues and Troubleshooting Tips

1. Installation Errors

- **Issue:** The WordPress installer fails to complete.
- **Solution:** Ensure your server meets WordPress's requirements (PHP version, database compatibility). Contact your hosting provider for support.

2. SSL Not Working

- **Issue:** SSL shows as inactive.
- **Solution:** Recheck SSL settings in your hosting dashboard and WordPress settings.

3. Slow Performance

- **Issue:** Website loads slowly after installation.
- **Solution:** Optimize images, use a caching plugin (e.g., WP Super Cache), and choose a reliable hosting provider.

Summary

Establishing a solid WordPress environment is the first step to creating a successful WooCommerce store. By selecting the right hosting provider, registering a memorable domain, and properly installing WordPress, you lay the groundwork for a high-performing e-commerce website.

Key Takeaways:

1. **Choose Reliable Hosting:** Factors like performance, scalability, and support are critical.
2. **Pick a Strong Domain Name:** Your domain is your store's identity—keep it relevant and simple.
3. **Install WordPress Correctly:** Use one-click installers or manual methods for setup.
4. **Optimize Configuration:** Secure your site with SSL, set up SEO-friendly permalinks, and install essential plugins.
5. **Test and Troubleshoot:** Ensure your site performs well before adding WooCommerce.

With your WordPress environment ready, the next chapter will focus on installing and configuring WooCommerce to turn your website into a thriving online store.

Chapter 4: Navigating the WordPress Dashboard: Your Command Center

The WordPress dashboard is your central hub for managing every aspect of your website, from content creation to plugin management. Mastering this interface is crucial for effectively running your online store and ensuring a seamless user experience for your customers. This chapter provides a comprehensive guide to navigating the WordPress dashboard, explaining its key components, functions, and tools to optimize your workflow.

Understanding the WordPress Dashboard

The WordPress dashboard is an intuitive, user-friendly interface designed to provide easy access to the features and settings of your site. When you log in to your WordPress site (yoursite.com/wp-admin), you're greeted with the dashboard, which is divided into several sections for efficient navigation and management.

The Main Areas of the Dashboard

1. **Admin Toolbar:** The horizontal bar at the top, offering quick links to common tasks like visiting the site or managing comments.
2. **Sidebar Menu:** The vertical menu on the left, which organizes all site management tools into categories.
3. **Main Workspace:** The central area where you'll perform tasks like writing posts or customizing settings.
4. **Footer:** Contains links to WordPress documentation and support.

Logging In and Customizing the Dashboard

Logging In

Access the dashboard by visiting yoursite.com/wp-admin and entering your username and password. For added security, consider using two-factor authentication or limiting login attempts with a plugin like Wordfence.

Customizing the Dashboard

Tailor the dashboard to fit your workflow by:

1. **Adding or Removing Widgets:** Click "Screen Options" (top-right) to toggle widgets like "At a Glance" or "Quick Draft."
2. **Rearranging Widgets:** Drag and drop widgets to arrange them in your preferred layout.
3. **Using Plugins for Enhancement:** Plugins like Adminimize allow further customization by enabling or disabling specific dashboard elements.

Exploring the Sidebar Menu

The sidebar menu organizes WordPress's features into categories for easy access. Here's a breakdown of the most important sections:

1. Dashboard

- **Home:** The landing page for updates, news, and quick stats about your site.
- **Updates:** View and apply updates to WordPress, plugins, or themes. Keeping everything updated is crucial for security and performance.

2. Posts

- Manage blog content like articles, announcements, or news.
- **Add New Post:** Opens the editor for creating content.
- **Categories:** Organize posts into groups for better navigation.
- **Tags:** Add keywords to improve searchability and SEO.

3. Media

- **Library:** Access and manage all uploaded images, videos, and other media files.
- **Add New:** Upload new media directly from your computer.
- Use optimized formats and compression to ensure fast loading times.

4. Pages

- Similar to posts but typically used for static content like "About Us" or "Contact" pages.
- Pages are hierarchical, allowing parent-child relationships for organization.

5. Comments

- Moderate and respond to user comments.
- Use plugins like Akismet to filter spam.

6. Appearance

Customize your site's design and layout.

- **Themes:** Choose or upload a theme to define the look of your site.
- **Customize:** Access the WordPress Customizer for real-time design adjustments.
- **Widgets:** Manage sidebar or footer content, like menus or search bars.
- **Menus:** Create and organize navigation menus for your site.

7. Plugins

- **Installed Plugins:** View, activate, deactivate, or delete plugins.
- **Add New:** Search for and install new plugins to add functionality.
- Regularly update plugins to avoid security vulnerabilities.

8. Users

- Manage user accounts with different roles (e.g., Admin, Editor, Subscriber).
- Add or edit user profiles, including passwords and permissions.

9. Tools

- Access import/export tools for transferring content.
- Use the "Site Health" feature to analyze your website's performance and security.

10. Settings

- **General:** Adjust site title, tagline, and time zone.
- **Reading:** Set how posts and pages appear on your site.
- **Permalinks:** Customize URL structures for SEO and readability.

Working with the Admin Toolbar

The admin toolbar at the top of the dashboard offers shortcuts for common tasks. Key features include:

- **Visit Site:** Quickly navigate between the backend and the live view of your site.
- **New:** Create new posts, pages, or other content with a single click.
- **Edit Page/Post:** Directly edit the page or post you're viewing on the live site.
- **Updates:** Access the updates center to ensure your WordPress installation is current.

Managing Content: Posts, Pages, and Media

Creating and Editing Posts

1. Navigate to **Posts > Add New** to open the WordPress editor.
2. Enter a title and use the content area to write and format your post.
3. Add categories and tags for organization.
4. Set a featured image to represent the post visually.
5. Preview your work before publishing.

Creating and Editing Pages

1. Go to **Pages > Add New.**
2. Use the editor to add static content, such as an "About Us" page.
3. Publish or save as a draft for later.

Managing Media

1. Access the Media Library to view all uploaded files.
2. Add ALT text to images for better SEO and accessibility.
3. Delete unused media to free up storage space.

Using the WordPress Customizer

The WordPress Customizer allows you to preview changes to your site in real time. Access it by navigating to **Appearance > Customize.**
Key Features:

- **Site Identity:** Update your site title, tagline, and logo.
- **Colors:** Adjust your theme's color palette.
- **Menus:** Create and assign navigation menus.
- **Widgets:** Add or modify widgets in sidebars or footers.
- **Additional CSS:** Insert custom CSS for advanced styling.

Optimizing Your Workflow with Plugins

Plugins extend WordPress's functionality, enabling you to customize your dashboard and site. Recommended plugins for improving workflow:

- **Elementor:** Drag-and-drop page builder for creating visually appealing pages.
- **Jetpack:** All-in-one plugin for performance, security, and design tools.
- **WPForms:** Simple form builder for creating contact forms or surveys.
- **Rank Math:** Advanced SEO plugin for optimizing content.

Troubleshooting Dashboard Issues

1. Slow Dashboard

- **Cause:** Too many plugins or limited server resources.
- **Solution:** Deactivate unnecessary plugins and upgrade hosting if needed.

2. Missing Features

- **Cause:** User roles or incomplete installations.
- **Solution:** Check user permissions or reinstall WordPress core files.

3. Error Messages

- **Cause:** Conflicts between plugins or themes.

- **Solution:** Temporarily deactivate plugins to identify the source of the conflict.

Summary

The WordPress dashboard serves as your command center, providing access to all the tools and settings required to manage your website effectively. By understanding its structure, customizing it to fit your needs, and leveraging its features, you can streamline your workflow and focus on growing your online store.

Key Takeaways:

- Familiarize yourself with the sidebar menu to efficiently access site management tools.
- Use the WordPress Customizer to make real-time adjustments to your site's design.
- Leverage plugins to extend dashboard functionality and enhance user experience.
- Regularly update WordPress, themes, and plugins to maintain performance and security.
- Troubleshoot common issues like slow performance or missing features to keep your site running smoothly.

With a strong grasp of the dashboard, you're well-equipped to manage your WordPress site confidently. In the next chapter, we'll dive into installing and configuring WooCommerce, transforming your website into a fully functional online store.

Chapter 5: Installing and Configuring WooCommerce: A Step-by-Step Guide

WooCommerce is the backbone of your WordPress-powered e-commerce store. Installing and configuring it properly is the first step to transforming your website into a fully functional online store. This chapter provides a detailed walkthrough to help you install, set up, and optimize WooCommerce for a seamless shopping experience.

Why WooCommerce?

WooCommerce is a free and open-source plugin that integrates seamlessly with WordPress, enabling you to sell products or services online. Its flexibility, scalability, and extensive ecosystem of extensions make it a top choice for e-commerce entrepreneurs. By following this step-by-step guide, you'll be ready to set up your store efficiently and tailor it to your unique business needs.

Step 1: Installing WooCommerce

1. Accessing the Plugin Repository

1. Log in to your WordPress dashboard.
2. Navigate to **Plugins > Add New.**
3. In the search bar, type **WooCommerce.**

2. Installing WooCommerce

1. Once WooCommerce appears in the search results, click the **Install Now** button.
2. Wait for the installation to complete, then click **Activate.**

3. Plugin Activation

Upon activation, WooCommerce automatically launches its setup wizard, guiding you through the initial configuration.

Step 2: The WooCommerce Setup Wizard

The setup wizard simplifies the configuration process, ensuring that your store's basic settings are in place.

1. Store Details

Enter the essential details of your business:

- Store Address: Your physical location (or primary business address).
- Currency: Choose the currency for your store's transactions.
- Selling Locations: Specify where you'll sell your products.

- Shipping Locations: Define regions where you'll ship orders.

2. Industry

Select your store's industry, such as fashion, electronics, or health and beauty. This helps WooCommerce recommend relevant features and extensions.

3. Product Type

Indicate the type of products you'll sell:

- Physical Products: Items that require shipping.
- Digital Products: Downloads like eBooks or software.
- Services: Offerings like consultations or memberships.

4. Business Details

- Indicate whether you're setting up a new store or migrating an existing one.
- Choose optional WooCommerce features, such as automated tax calculations or product recommendations.

5. Theme Selection

WooCommerce will recommend themes optimized for e-commerce. You can:

- Choose a free WooCommerce-compatible theme (e.g., Storefront).
- Upload a custom theme you've purchased or developed.

Step 3: Configuring Core WooCommerce Settings

1. General Settings

Access these settings under **WooCommerce > Settings > General.**

- **Store Address:** Ensure your address details are accurate.
- **Selling Locations:** Select whether you'll sell worldwide or to specific countries.
- **Currency Options:** Define the currency format for your region.

2. Product Settings

Navigate to **WooCommerce > Settings > Products.**

- **Shop Page:** Assign a page to serve as your main shop display.
- **Weight and Dimensions:** Set default units for product weight and size.
- **Inventory:** Enable stock management to automatically track product availability.

3. Tax Settings

If you enabled tax calculations during setup, configure them under **WooCommerce > Settings > Tax.**

- **Enable Taxes:** Ensure the checkbox for taxes is ticked.
- **Tax Rates:** Add standard and reduced tax rates based on your selling regions.

4. Shipping Settings

Set up shipping zones and methods under **WooCommerce > Settings > Shipping.**

- **Shipping Zones:** Define regions where specific shipping methods apply.
- **Shipping Methods:** Add options like flat rate, free shipping, or local pickup.

5. Payments

WooCommerce supports multiple payment gateways. Configure them under **WooCommerce > Settings > Payments.**

- **PayPal:** Set up your PayPal account for secure online transactions.
- **Stripe:** Accept credit card payments directly on your site.
- **Direct Bank Transfer:** Offer offline payment options.

Step 4: Adding Products to Your Store

1. Adding Your First Product

1. Navigate to **Products > Add New.**
2. Enter the product name and description in the editor.
3. Set the **Product Data** type:
    - **Simple Product:** A single item with no variations.
    - **Variable Product:** Items with variations, such as size or color.
    - **Grouped Product:** A collection of related items sold together.
    - **Downloadable Product:** Digital files available for download.

2. Key Product Fields

- **Price:** Enter the regular and sale price.
- **Inventory:** Define stock quantity and SKU (stock keeping unit).
- **Shipping:** Add weight and dimensions for physical products.
- **Linked Products:** Suggest upsells and cross-sells to increase sales.

3. Product Images

- **Featured Image:** The primary image displayed on your product page.
- **Gallery:** Additional images to showcase your product from different angles.

4. Publishing Products

Click **Publish** to make your product live. Use the **Preview** button to check how it appears on your store.

Step 5: Customizing Your WooCommerce Store

1. Optimizing the Shop Page

- Access the shop page under **Appearance** > **Customize** > **WooCommerce.**
- Arrange product categories and filters for a user-friendly browsing experience.

2. Configuring the Checkout Process

- Simplify the checkout process by reducing the number of steps.
- Enable guest checkout to avoid forcing customers to create an account.

3. Adding a Secure Payment Gateway

- Install SSL (Secure Socket Layer) to encrypt transactions.
- Test payment methods to ensure seamless functionality.

4. Using Widgets and Shortcodes

WooCommerce includes widgets and shortcodes for displaying products and categories on any page or post.

Step 6: Installing Essential WooCommerce Plugins

Enhance your store's functionality with these must-have plugins:

1. **WooCommerce SEO:** Improve product visibility in search engines.
2. **WooCommerce Subscriptions:** Add recurring billing options.
3. **WooCommerce Bookings:** Allow customers to book appointments or reservations.
4. **Advanced Coupons:** Offer discounts, BOGO deals, and gift cards.
5. **WooCommerce Analytics:** Track sales, product performance, and customer behavior.

Step 7: Testing Your WooCommerce Store

Before launching, thoroughly test your store:

1. **Product Pages:** Ensure descriptions, images, and prices are correct.
2. **Checkout Process:** Test various payment methods to identify errors.
3. **Shipping Calculations:** Verify shipping costs are accurate for different locations.

4. **Mobile Responsiveness:** Check how your store appears and functions on smartphones and tablets.

Common Issues and Troubleshooting Tips

1. Plugin Conflicts

- **Issue:** Errors or slow performance after installing WooCommerce.
- **Solution:** Deactivate other plugins to identify conflicts.

2. Payment Gateway Issues

- **Issue:** Payment methods not working as expected.
- **Solution:** Double-check API keys and credentials for gateways like PayPal or Stripe.

3. Tax Calculation Errors

- **Issue:** Taxes are not applied correctly.
- **Solution:** Review tax rate tables and ensure geolocation is enabled.

Summary

Installing and configuring WooCommerce is a straightforward process that lays the groundwork for a successful online store. By following this step-by-step guide, you'll ensure your store is functional, secure, and tailored to your business needs.

Key Takeaways:

1. Install WooCommerce via the WordPress plugin repository.
2. Use the setup wizard to configure basic settings for your store.
3. Add and optimize products with detailed descriptions, images, and pricing.
4. Customize your shop page, checkout process, and payment gateways for a seamless user experience.
5. Test your store thoroughly before launching to ensure a smooth customer journey.

With WooCommerce installed and configured, you're ready to begin selling online. The next chapter will explore advanced customization and tools to optimize your e-commerce store for growth.

Chapter 6: Understanding WooCommerce Settings: Tailoring Your Store's Core Features

WooCommerce is a powerful e-commerce platform with extensive settings to customize your store. Mastering these settings is essential to tailor your store to meet business needs and provide an excellent user experience. In this chapter, we'll explore the various WooCommerce settings and their configurations, helping you fine-tune your store's core features.

The Importance of WooCommerce Settings

WooCommerce settings form the backbone of your online store. These options allow you to:

- Define how products are displayed.
- Configure shipping, taxes, and payment gateways.
- Manage customer accounts and checkout processes.
- Ensure compliance with legal and regional requirements.

By understanding these settings, you can ensure your store operates efficiently and delivers a seamless experience for customers.

Navigating WooCommerce Settings

To access WooCommerce settings:

1. Log in to your WordPress dashboard.
2. Navigate to **WooCommerce > Settings.**
3. Use the tabs at the top to explore different sections, such as General, Products, Shipping, Payments, Accounts & Privacy, and Emails.

---

1. General Settings

The General tab covers foundational store configurations:

Store Address

- Enter your business address.
- This information determines tax calculations and shipping origins.

Selling Locations

- Choose where your store will sell products:
    - **Sell to all countries.**
    - **Sell to specific countries.**

- This setting ensures your store complies with regional restrictions or preferences.

Shipping Locations

- Define where you'll ship products.
- Options include shipping globally, to specific regions, or disabling shipping entirely.

Currency Options

- Set the currency format for your store:
    - Currency (e.g., USD, EUR).
    - Currency position (left, right, etc.).
    - Thousand separator and decimal settings.

Additional Options

- Enable or disable taxes and coupons.
- Decide if customers must enter an address during checkout.

---

2. Product Settings

The Products tab allows you to control how products are displayed and managed.

Shop Pages

- **Shop Page:** Assign the primary page where all products are displayed.
- **Redirect to Cart:** Automatically direct customers to the cart after adding a product.

Measurements

- Define the default unit for weight (e.g., kg, lb) and dimensions (e.g., cm, in).
- These settings are essential for accurate shipping calculations.

Inventory Management

- Enable stock management to track product availability.
- Set low stock and out-of-stock thresholds to receive notifications.
- Determine whether stock is reduced automatically after orders.

Downloadable Products

- Set access restrictions for digital products.
- Choose whether customers need an account to download purchases.

---

3. Tax Settings

Tax regulations vary by region, and WooCommerce's tax settings ensure compliance:

Enable Taxes

- Tick the **Enable Taxes** box to activate tax calculation.

Tax Classes

- Define classes like **Standard Rate**, **Reduced Rate**, and **Zero Rate.**
- Use these to apply different tax rules to specific products or regions.

Tax Display Settings

- Choose whether prices include or exclude taxes on product pages and at checkout.
- Display tax totals as single values or itemized lists.

Geolocation

- Use geolocation to calculate taxes based on the customer's location automatically.

---

4. Shipping Settings

Shipping is a critical aspect of e-commerce. WooCommerce offers flexible options for configuring shipping zones, methods, and rates:

Shipping Zones

- Create zones for specific regions, such as countries, states, or postal codes.
- Assign shipping methods (flat rate, free shipping, or local pickup) to each zone.

Shipping Classes

- Group products with similar shipping requirements.
- Example: Assign heavy items to a "Heavy Goods" class for specialized rates.

Shipping Methods

- **Flat Rate:** Set a fixed cost per order or product.
- **Free Shipping:** Offer free shipping based on criteria like minimum order value.
- **Local Pickup:** Allow customers to collect orders from a specified location.

Shipping Calculations

- Enable shipping cost display during the checkout process.

---

5. Payments Settings

WooCommerce supports multiple payment gateways. Proper configuration ensures secure and seamless transactions.

Popular Payment Gateways

- **PayPal:** Secure, globally accepted, and easy to set up.
- **Stripe:** Allows credit card payments directly on your site.
- **Direct Bank Transfer (BACS):** Suitable for offline payments.
- **Cash on Delivery:** Ideal for local orders.

Setting Up Payment Gateways

1. Navigate to **WooCommerce > Settings > Payments.**
2. Activate desired payment methods.
3. Configure settings for each gateway, such as account details and payment instructions.

---

6. Accounts & Privacy Settings

Customer accounts and privacy settings play a vital role in user experience and compliance:

Account Options

- Enable or disable guest checkout.
- Allow customers to create accounts during checkout or registration.
- Automatically generate usernames and passwords for new accounts.

Privacy Settings

- Define how long personal data is retained for orders, accounts, and inactivity.
- Display privacy policies during registration and checkout to comply with regulations like GDPR.

---

7. Emails Settings

WooCommerce sends various transactional emails to customers and administrators. You can customize these emails for branding and clarity:

Email Notifications

- Examples of notifications:
  - New Order
  - Completed Order
  - Refund Processed
- Activate or deactivate specific notifications based on your preferences.

Customizing Email Templates

- Access **WooCommerce > Settings > Emails.**
- Modify the sender's name and address.
- Use the built-in editor to change email layouts, colors, and content.

---

8. Integration and Advanced Settings

Integration

- Connect WooCommerce with third-party tools like Google Analytics or Facebook Pixel.
- Use APIs for advanced integrations with CRM systems or external apps.

Advanced Settings

- Control REST API permissions for developers.
- Manage WooCommerce system status and logs to troubleshoot issues.
- Set up account endpoints to define URL structures for user actions.

Common WooCommerce Settings Challenges

1. Incorrect Tax Calculations

- **Cause:** Misconfigured tax rates or geolocation issues.
- **Solution:** Double-check tax tables and enable geolocation.

2. Shipping Errors

- **Cause:** Overlapping zones or missing rates.
- **Solution:** Review shipping zones and assign methods to each.

3. Payment Gateway Failures

- **Cause:** Incorrect API keys or integration problems.
- **Solution:** Verify gateway credentials and test payment flows.

Optimizing WooCommerce Settings for Success

To ensure a smooth operation, consider the following tips:

- Regularly review and update tax and shipping rates.
- Test all payment methods after configuration.
- Monitor email deliverability to avoid missed notifications.

- Use plugins like **WooCommerce Booster** or **Advanced WooCommerce** for enhanced settings control.

Summary

Understanding and configuring WooCommerce settings is a critical step in building a successful online store. By mastering these options, you can create a tailored shopping experience that meets customer expectations and aligns with your business goals.

Key Takeaways:

1. General settings define your store's location, currency, and selling regions.
2. Product settings manage inventory, measurements, and downloadable products.
3. Tax and shipping settings ensure compliance and operational efficiency.
4. Payment settings provide secure, flexible transaction options.
5. Privacy and account settings enhance user experience while maintaining legal compliance.
6. Email notifications keep customers and administrators informed about orders.

With these settings optimized, your WooCommerce store will be equipped to deliver exceptional service and maximize conversions. In the next chapter, we'll dive into creating compelling product pages that attract and engage your audience.

Chapter 7: Choosing the Perfect Theme for Your Store: Design That Converts

In e-commerce, first impressions are everything. Your store's theme is the cornerstone of that initial impression, shaping how customers perceive your brand and interact with your site. A theme not only dictates your store's visual appeal but also impacts usability, performance, and, most importantly, conversion rates.

This chapter will guide you through the process of choosing the perfect theme for your WooCommerce store. From understanding the role of themes in e-commerce success to exploring practical considerations and implementation steps, you'll gain all the knowledge needed to create a store that looks great and drives sales.

The Importance of Choosing the Right Theme

Your store's theme serves as its foundation, defining its structure, style, and functionality. Beyond mere aesthetics, a well-designed theme enhances user experience (UX), builds trust, and fosters customer loyalty.

Key Benefits of a Great Theme

1. **Brand Representation:** Your theme reflects your business's identity, setting the tone for customer interaction.
2. **User-Friendly Navigation:** An intuitive layout ensures visitors can find products easily, reducing frustration.
3. **Performance Optimization:** A lightweight theme loads faster, improving user retention and SEO rankings.
4. **Responsive Design:** Mobile-friendly themes cater to customers browsing on various devices, a crucial factor in today's market.

What to Look for in a WooCommerce Theme

Choosing the right theme requires balancing design, functionality, and performance. Here are critical factors to consider:

1. WooCommerce Compatibility

Ensure the theme is explicitly designed for WooCommerce. Themes built for e-commerce integrate seamlessly with WooCommerce features, like product pages, carts, and checkout systems.

2. Mobile Responsiveness

Mobile commerce accounts for a significant portion of online sales. Your theme must adapt to various screen sizes, ensuring smooth navigation and functionality on smartphones and tablets.

3. Speed and Performance

Slow-loading websites deter customers and harm your SEO rankings. Choose themes with lightweight, optimized code to ensure quick load times.

4. Customization Options

Your store should reflect your brand's identity. Look for themes offering flexibility in:

- Fonts
- Colors
- Layouts
- Header and footer designs

5. SEO Optimization

A good theme incorporates SEO best practices, such as structured data, clean HTML markup, and fast load times, boosting your store's visibility in search engine results.

6. Regular Updates and Support

Themes should be updated frequently to maintain compatibility with the latest WordPress and WooCommerce versions. Opt for themes backed by active developers and robust customer support.

7. Demo Content Availability

Pre-built demo content allows you to visualize and set up your store quickly, providing a head start in customization.

Top WooCommerce Themes for E-Commerce Stores

1. Storefront

- **Description:** The official WooCommerce theme designed for simplicity and seamless integration.
- **Best For:** Beginners or minimalist stores.
- **Features:** Lightweight, customizable, and supported by WooCommerce developers.

2. Astra

- **Description:** A fast, highly customizable theme compatible with major page builders.
- **Best For:** Stores needing versatility and unique branding.
- **Features:** Pre-designed templates, optimized performance, and drag-and-drop functionality.

3. Flatsome

- **Description:** Known for its modern, sleek design and built-in page builder.
- **Best For:** Visually appealing stores with interactive layouts.
- **Features:** Responsive design, customizable headers, and live theme options.

4. OceanWP

- **Description:** A multipurpose theme with extensive WooCommerce features.
- **Best For:** Stores catering to diverse industries.
- **Features:** Fast loading, extensive customization, and full responsiveness.

5. Divi

- **Description:** A premium theme offering a powerful visual page builder.
- **Best For:** Creative stores emphasizing standout designs.
- **Features:** Drag-and-drop builder, global elements, and responsive editing.

Design Principles for High-Converting Themes

Once you've chosen a theme, aligning it with proven design principles can optimize your store's performance.

1. Simplicity

Keep the design clean and uncluttered. Overwhelming visitors with too many elements can distract them from making a purchase.

2. Visual Hierarchy

Use colors, typography, and white space strategically to emphasize important elements like call-to-action (CTA) buttons and featured products.

3. Navigation

A clear and intuitive navigation structure ensures customers can easily browse products and categories. Include a search bar and breadcrumbs for added convenience.

4. Trust Signals

Incorporate elements like:

- Customer reviews
- Secure payment icons
- Return policy highlights

These build credibility and reduce purchase anxiety.

5. Mobile Optimization

Test how your site appears on mobile devices. Ensure fast loading times, touch-friendly buttons, and a seamless checkout process.

How to Install and Customize Your Theme

Step 1: Install the Theme

1. Go to your WordPress Dashboard.
2. Navigate to **Appearance** > **Themes** > **Add New.**
3. Search for the desired theme or upload it if it's a premium option.
4. Click **Install** and then **Activate.**

Step 2: Import Demo Content

Many themes come with demo content to help you visualize your store's design. Use this feature if available:

- Go to the theme's settings.
- Locate the **Demo Import** option.
- Select a demo design and follow the instructions.

Step 3: Customize the Theme

Access the WordPress Customizer via **Appearance** > **Customize:**

- **Site Identity:** Upload your logo and set a tagline.
- **Colors:** Match your branding palette.
- **Typography:** Adjust font styles for readability.
- **Header and Footer:** Add navigation links and contact details.
- **Widgets:** Include product categories, search bars, and other useful elements.

Step 4: Test Your Design

Before launching, test your store for:

- Responsiveness on different devices.
- Browser compatibility.
- Loading speed using tools like Google PageSpeed Insights.

Common Mistakes to Avoid When Choosing Themes

1. Prioritizing Looks Over Functionality

A beautiful theme is useless if it doesn't support essential e-commerce features. Balance aesthetics with functionality.

2. Ignoring Speed and Performance

Themes with excessive features or bloated code can slow down your site. Opt for lightweight themes focused on performance.

3. Skipping Updates

Failing to update themes can lead to compatibility issues and security vulnerabilities.

4. Overloading with Features

Themes with unnecessary features may complicate navigation and confuse visitors. Keep it simple and focused on your store's goals.

Case Study: A Theme That Boosted Sales

Consider an online boutique that switched from a generic theme to Flatsome. After implementing the new theme:

- Page load times decreased by 40%.
- Bounce rates dropped by 25%.
- Sales increased by 15% within three months due to improved user experience and aesthetic appeal.

This highlights how choosing the right theme can directly impact your bottom line.

Summary

A well-chosen theme can elevate your WooCommerce store from a functional website to an engaging, conversion-driven platform.

Key Takeaways

1. Select a WooCommerce-compatible theme that's responsive, fast, and customizable.
2. Prioritize UX principles like simplicity, clear navigation, and mobile optimization.
3. Test and refine your theme to ensure it aligns with your brand identity and business goals.
4. Avoid pitfalls such as bloated features or outdated themes.

By investing time and effort into selecting the perfect theme, you create a solid foundation for e-commerce success. In the next chapter, we'll explore the art of creating compelling product pages that engage customers and drive purchases.

Chapter 8: Customizing Your WooCommerce Store: Plugins and Page Builders

Customization is the key to transforming a functional WooCommerce store into a unique shopping destination that reflects your brand and captivates your audience. While WooCommerce provides a strong foundation, plugins and page builders empower you to enhance your store's functionality and aesthetics effortlessly.

This chapter explores how to leverage plugins and page builders to customize your WooCommerce store. From essential plugins to advanced page builders, you'll learn how to create a store that stands out in a competitive e-commerce landscape.

Why Customize Your WooCommerce Store?

Customization allows you to tailor your store to meet specific business goals and customer expectations.

Key Benefits

1. **Brand Differentiation:** Stand out from competitors with a unique design and features.
2. **Enhanced User Experience:** Improve navigation, product discovery, and checkout processes.
3. **Scalability:** Add functionality as your business grows.
4. **Higher Conversions:** A personalized shopping experience can lead to increased sales.

Essential Plugins for WooCommerce Customization

Plugins are add-ons that extend WooCommerce's functionality. Selecting the right plugins ensures your store runs efficiently while providing additional features.

1. WooCommerce Product Add-Ons

- **Purpose:** Allows customers to customize products (e.g., adding engravings or selecting options).
- **Benefits:** Enhances the shopping experience with personalized options.

2. WooCommerce Subscriptions

- **Purpose:** Enables subscription-based sales for recurring revenue.
- **Benefits:** Ideal for businesses offering memberships, digital products, or regular deliveries.

3. WooCommerce Bookings

- **Purpose:** Allows customers to book appointments or rentals directly through your store.
- **Benefits:** Great for service-based businesses or rental companies.

4. Yoast SEO

- **Purpose:** Optimizes your store for search engines.

- **Benefits:** Improves visibility and drives organic traffic.

5. WPForms

- **Purpose:** Adds contact forms, survey forms, or payment forms.
- **Benefits:** Simplifies customer interactions and data collection.

6. Smush

- **Purpose:** Compresses and optimizes images without losing quality.
- **Benefits:** Improves site speed and performance.

7. Jetpack

- **Purpose:** Offers security, performance, and marketing tools in one plugin.
- **Benefits:** An all-in-one solution for managing various aspects of your store.

8. Mailchimp for WooCommerce

- **Purpose:** Syncs customer data for targeted email marketing campaigns.
- **Benefits:** Boosts engagement and drives repeat purchases.

The Role of Page Builders in WooCommerce Customization

Page builders simplify the process of designing and customizing your store without requiring coding knowledge.

Why Use Page Builders?

- **Ease of Use:** Drag-and-drop functionality makes customization accessible.
- **Design Flexibility:** Create visually stunning pages tailored to your brand.
- **Integration:** Many builders seamlessly integrate with WooCommerce.

Popular Page Builders for WooCommerce

1. Elementor

- **Features:** Drag-and-drop interface, WooCommerce widgets, and pre-built templates.
- **Best For:** Users looking for creative freedom and ease of use.
- **Standout Feature:** WooCommerce Builder for designing product pages, carts, and checkouts.

2. WPBakery

- **Features:** Backend and frontend editing, pre-designed elements, and extensive add-ons.
- **Best For:** Advanced users requiring detailed customization options.

- **Standout Feature:** Grid builder for unique layouts.

3. Beaver Builder

- **Features:** Intuitive interface, responsive design tools, and WooCommerce module support.
- **Best For:** Beginners seeking a straightforward page-building experience.
- **Standout Feature:** Live editing for real-time design adjustments.

4. Divi Builder

- **Features:** Visual editing, pre-designed templates, and global elements.
- **Best For:** Users wanting visually appealing and consistent designs.
- **Standout Feature:** Theme Builder for customizing headers, footers, and body content.

5. Gutenberg (WordPress Block Editor)

- **Features:** Built-in block editor for WordPress, offering basic customization.
- **Best For:** Minimalists preferring lightweight, no-frills editing.
- **Standout Feature:** Core integration with WordPress.

How to Customize Your WooCommerce Store Using Plugins and Page Builders

Step 1: Identify Customization Goals

Determine what aspects of your store you want to enhance:

- **Design:** Improve layout, typography, and imagery.
- **Functionality:** Add features like dynamic pricing, product filters, or advanced shipping options.
- **Performance:** Optimize for speed, SEO, and mobile responsiveness.

Step 2: Choose the Right Tools

1. Research plugins and page builders that align with your goals.
2. Check reviews, ratings, and compatibility with WooCommerce.
3. Opt for tools with regular updates and strong developer support.

Step 3: Install and Activate Plugins

1. Go to your WordPress dashboard.
2. Navigate to **Plugins > Add New.**
3. Search for the desired plugin, click **Install**, and then **Activate.**

Step 4: Design with a Page Builder

1. Install your preferred page builder.

2. Create custom pages, such as:
    - **Home Page:** Showcase featured products, categories, and promotions.
    - **Product Pages:** Highlight key features, benefits, and CTAs.
    - **Checkout Page:** Simplify steps to reduce cart abandonment.
3. Use widgets and modules to add WooCommerce-specific elements like product grids, cart totals, or customer reviews.

Step 5: Test and Optimize

1. Ensure your customizations work seamlessly across devices.
2. Use performance tools to test site speed and responsiveness.
3. Gather feedback from users to refine your store.

Best Practices for Customizing Your Store

1. **Prioritize User Experience**
   Every customization should enhance navigation, readability, or purchase convenience.
2. **Maintain Consistency**
   Ensure fonts, colors, and branding elements are consistent across pages.
3. **Avoid Plugin Overload**
   Using too many plugins can slow your site. Install only what you need.
4. **Regularly Update Plugins and Page Builders**
   Outdated tools can cause compatibility issues and security risks.
5. **Backup Your Site**
   Before making significant changes, create a backup to safeguard your data.

Case Study: Customization Success Story

A boutique fashion store used Elementor and essential WooCommerce plugins to revamp its website:

- **Challenges:** The default theme lacked flexibility for showcasing high-end products.
- **Customizations:**
    - Elementor's WooCommerce Builder to create stunning product pages.
    - WooCommerce Product Add-Ons for personalized monogramming options.
    - Mailchimp for targeted email campaigns.
- **Results:**
    - Conversion rates increased by 20%.

- Average session duration rose by 30%.
- Customer satisfaction improved due to a more seamless shopping experience.

Summary

Customizing your WooCommerce store with plugins and page builders is an effective way to enhance functionality, design, and user experience.

Key Takeaways

1. Plugins extend WooCommerce's capabilities, adding essential features like subscriptions, bookings, and SEO tools.
2. Page builders like Elementor and Divi simplify the design process, enabling stunning, responsive layouts.
3. Always prioritize user experience, performance, and scalability when customizing your store.
4. Test your customizations thoroughly to ensure they meet customer expectations and business goals.

With the right tools and strategies, you can create a WooCommerce store that not only attracts customers but also converts them into loyal buyers. In the next chapter, we'll focus on creating high-converting product pages that showcase your offerings and encourage purchases.

Chapter 9: Adding Products: Simple, Variable, Digital, and More

The products you offer are the heart of your WooCommerce store. Whether you're selling physical goods, digital downloads, or services, WooCommerce provides flexible tools to list and manage them effectively. Adding products might seem straightforward, but understanding the nuances of product types can help you optimize listings for better conversions and customer experience.

This chapter provides a comprehensive guide to adding products to your WooCommerce store, covering everything from simple and variable products to more advanced types like grouped and virtual products.

Understanding Product Types in WooCommerce

WooCommerce categorizes products into various types to cater to different business needs. Let's briefly overview the key product types before diving into how to add them.

1. Simple Products

- **Definition:** Basic, standalone items without options.
- **Examples:** A book, a coffee mug, or a single subscription plan.

2. Variable Products

- **Definition:** Products with multiple variations, each having unique attributes like size, color, or material.
- **Examples:** T-shirts in different sizes and colors.

3. Digital Products

- **Definition:** Downloadable items like eBooks, software, or music files.
- **Examples:** A PDF guide or a music album.

4. Grouped Products

- **Definition:** A collection of related products displayed together.
- **Examples:** A set of books sold individually or as a bundle.

5. Virtual Products

- **Definition:** Non-physical products that don't require shipping.
- **Examples:** Online courses or consultations.

6. Subscription Products

- **Definition:** Products billed periodically, such as memberships or subscription boxes.
- **Examples:** Monthly fitness plans or recurring product deliveries.

How to Add Products to Your WooCommerce Store

Step 1: Navigate to the Product Section

1. Go to your WordPress dashboard.
2. Select **Products > Add New.**

Step 2: Fill Out the Basic Details

- **Product Name:** Choose a clear, descriptive title.
- **Description:** Write a detailed description that highlights key features and benefits. Use formatting (headings, bullet points) to make it easy to read.

Step 3: Set the Product Data

The **Product Data** section is where you configure the product type and attributes.

Adding a Simple Product

1. **Select Product Type:** In the Product Data dropdown, choose **Simple Product.**
2. **General Tab:**
   - Set the **Regular Price** and **Sale Price** (optional).
   - If it's a digital product, enable the **Downloadable** and/or **Virtual** options.
3. **Inventory Tab:**
   - Enter the **SKU** (Stock Keeping Unit) for unique product identification.
   - Manage stock levels and enable stock notifications if needed.
4. **Shipping Tab:**
   - Add product dimensions (weight, height, width).
   - Choose a shipping class if applicable.
5. **Linked Products Tab:**
   - Set up upsells (higher-end products) and cross-sells (related products).
6. **Attributes and Variations:** Not applicable for simple products.
7. **Advanced Tab:**
   - Add a purchase note (e.g., "Thank you for your order!").
   - Enable reviews for customer feedback.

Adding a Variable Product

Variable products allow you to offer variations under a single product listing.

1. **Select Product Type:** Choose **Variable Product** from the Product Data dropdown.
2. **Attributes Tab:**
   - Create attributes like size or color.
   - Check the **Used for variations** box.
3. **Variations Tab:**
   - Click **Add Variation** to set up individual options.
   - Configure prices, stock, and other details for each variation.
4. **Save Changes:** Ensure all variations are saved before publishing the product.

Adding Digital Products

Digital products require fewer settings since they don't involve shipping.

1. **Enable Downloadable Option:** Under the General tab, check the **Downloadable** option.
2. **Add Downloadable Files:** Upload the file(s) for the product.
3. **Set Download Limits:** Specify the number of downloads allowed per purchase or leave unlimited.
4. **Expiration Date:** Optionally set an expiry for downloads.

Adding Grouped Products

Grouped products are ideal for showcasing related items together.

1. **Select Product Type:** Choose **Grouped Product** from the dropdown.
2. **Add Linked Products:** In the Linked Products tab, search and select the items you want to group.
3. **Publish Grouped Product:** Customers can view and purchase individual items from the group.

Adding Virtual Products

Virtual products are non-physical items. These follow a similar process as simple products but without shipping details.

1. **Enable Virtual Option:** Check the **Virtual** box in the Product Data section.
2. **Skip Shipping Details:** No dimensions or shipping classes are required.

Optimizing Product Listings for Conversions

To maximize sales, your product listings need more than just technical accuracy—they need to appeal to your target audience.

1. Use High-Quality Images

- Display multiple angles and zoom options.
- Ensure images are optimized for fast loading without losing quality.

2. Write Compelling Product Descriptions

- Highlight features and benefits.
- Use persuasive language that connects with your audience's needs.

3. Optimize Titles and Tags

- Include relevant keywords for SEO.
- Make titles clear and specific.

4. Add Social Proof

- Display customer reviews and ratings.
- Include testimonials or case studies if available.

5. Include Product Videos

- Demonstrate product use cases or unique features.
- Embed YouTube or Vimeo videos for added engagement.

Common Mistakes to Avoid

1. **Skipping Detailed Descriptions:** Vague or generic descriptions can deter customers.
2. **Low-Quality Images:** Poor visuals reduce trust and appeal.
3. **Ignoring Stock Management:** Not tracking inventory can lead to overselling or missed opportunities.
4. **Neglecting SEO:** Without proper keywords and metadata, your products may not rank in search results.
5. **Incomplete Product Data:** Missing pricing, variations, or attributes can confuse customers.

Case Study: Effective Product Listing

An online electronics store transformed its listings by following best practices:

- **Before:** Basic descriptions, few images, and inconsistent pricing.
- **After:**

    - Descriptions emphasized benefits like durability and ease of use.
    - High-resolution images showed multiple angles.
    - SEO optimization increased product visibility.
- **Results:** The store saw a 30% increase in conversions within two months.

Summary

Adding and managing products in WooCommerce is a foundational skill for running an online store. By mastering the nuances of product types and applying best practices, you can create listings that attract and convert customers.

Key Takeaways

1. WooCommerce supports various product types, including simple, variable, digital, grouped, and virtual products.
2. Use the Product Data section to configure pricing, inventory, shipping, and other essential settings.
3. Optimize your listings with high-quality images, compelling descriptions, and SEO-friendly titles.
4. Avoid common mistakes like incomplete data, poor visuals, or neglecting SEO.

With a well-organized catalog of products, your WooCommerce store is primed for success. In the next chapter, we'll explore how to create high-converting product pages that drive sales and enhance user experience.

Chapter 10: Crafting Effective Product Descriptions and Images

Your product descriptions and images are your silent salespeople. They work tirelessly to showcase your offerings, communicate value, and persuade customers to click the "Buy Now" button. Crafting effective product descriptions and using compelling visuals is not just an art but a science that can significantly impact your WooCommerce store's conversion rates.

In this chapter, we'll explore the strategies and techniques to create persuasive product descriptions and choose visually appealing images that resonate with your audience.

The Role of Product Descriptions and Images in E-Commerce

Product descriptions and images are the primary ways customers interact with your products online.

Key Functions

1. **Informing Customers:** Provide essential details about the product.
2. **Building Trust:** High-quality images and well-written descriptions convey professionalism.
3. **Encouraging Purchases:** Persuasive content highlights benefits, not just features.
4. **Improving SEO:** Optimized descriptions and alt text for images help search engines rank your products.

Crafting Compelling Product Descriptions

1. Understand Your Target Audience

Before writing, know who you're talking to.

- **What are their pain points?** Identify problems your product solves.
- **What motivates them to buy?** Highlight how the product meets their needs.

2. Focus on Benefits, Not Just Features

While features describe the product, benefits explain why they matter to the customer.

- **Feature Example:** "Made from 100% organic cotton."
- **Benefit Example:** "Keeps your skin comfortable and eco-friendly, perfect for sensitive skin."

3. Use a Conversational Tone

Write as if you're speaking directly to your customer.

- Avoid overly formal language.
- Use words like "you" and "your" to make descriptions relatable.

4. Structure Descriptions for Readability

- **Headings and Subheadings:** Break up content into digestible sections.

- **Bullet Points:** Highlight key features and benefits for quick scanning.
- **Short Paragraphs:** Keep paragraphs concise to maintain attention.

5. Incorporate Power Words

Words like "exclusive," "limited," "reliable," and "proven" evoke emotions and drive urgency.

6. Add Social Proof

Include testimonials, awards, or mentions in media to boost credibility.

7. Optimize for SEO

- **Keywords:** Integrate relevant search terms naturally.
- **Meta Descriptions:** Write engaging snippets that appear in search results.
- **Long-Tail Keywords:** Target specific phrases your audience searches for.

Examples of Engaging Product Descriptions

Example 1: T-Shirt

- **Basic Description:**
  "This t-shirt is made of cotton."
- **Effective Description:**
  "Feel the ultimate comfort with our 100% organic cotton t-shirt. Designed for everyday wear, it's breathable, durable, and eco-friendly. Whether you're lounging at home or out on the go, this t-shirt is your perfect companion."

Example 2: Digital Course

- **Basic Description:**
  "Learn how to bake."
- **Effective Description:**
  "Transform your kitchen into a bakery with our step-by-step baking course! Perfect for beginners, you'll learn how to create mouthwatering bread, cakes, and pastries that rival professional bakers. Join 10,000+ happy students today!"

The Importance of High-Quality Product Images

Visuals play a vital role in online shopping, where customers can't physically touch or see the product.

Benefits of Great Product Images

1. **First Impressions:** High-quality images make your store appear professional.
2. **Better Understanding:** Showcase details like texture, color, and dimensions.
3. **Emotional Appeal:** Create desire and showcase lifestyle possibilities.

Tips for Capturing Effective Product Images

1. Use High-Resolution Photos

- Ensure images are sharp and clear.
- Avoid pixelation, especially on zoom-in features.

2. Show Multiple Angles

- Display front, back, and side views.
- Include close-ups of key details, like stitching or materials.

3. Include Lifestyle Shots

- Show the product in use to help customers visualize it in their lives.
- Example: A couch in a cozy living room setup.

4. Consistent Backgrounds

- Use a clean, neutral background for standard product images.
- White or light gray is ideal for most e-commerce stores.

5. Add Contextual Images

- Showcase product size or scale by placing it next to familiar objects.

6. Optimize for Speed

- Compress images to reduce loading times without compromising quality.
- Use tools like TinyPNG or ShortPixel for optimization.

Using Image Types Effectively

1. Primary Images

- Show the product prominently.
- This is the main image customers see in search results or categories.

2. Secondary Images

- Highlight specific features or variations.
- Example: Different colors of the same product.

3. Infographics

- Combine images with text to showcase features and benefits.
- Example: A diagram of a smartwatch's functionalities.

4. 360-Degree Images

- Allow customers to rotate and view products from all angles.
- Particularly useful for high-ticket items like furniture or electronics.

5. Videos

- Create short product demonstrations.
- Example: A blender making a smoothie in real-time.

Alt Text for Accessibility and SEO

Alt text serves two purposes: it makes your site accessible to visually impaired users and improves SEO.

Best Practices for Alt Text

1. **Be Descriptive:** Accurately describe what's in the image.
    - Example: "Red leather handbag with gold accents."
2. **Include Keywords:** Use relevant search terms naturally.
3. **Avoid Keyword Stuffing:** Don't overload alt text with irrelevant keywords.

Common Mistakes to Avoid

1. **Generic Descriptions:** Avoid vague phrases like "high quality" without specifics.
2. **Poor Image Quality:** Blurry or pixelated images can deter potential buyers.
3. **Misleading Visuals:** Ensure images accurately represent the product.
4. **Neglecting SEO:** Failing to optimize descriptions and images limits discoverability.
5. **Inconsistent Branding:** Keep fonts, colors, and image styles consistent.

Case Study: A Store's Transformation with Better Content

Scenario:

A WooCommerce store selling kitchen gadgets struggled with low sales despite offering competitive prices.

Issues Identified:

1. Generic product descriptions with no focus on benefits.
2. Low-resolution images that didn't showcase product details.

Changes Made:

1. Updated descriptions to highlight benefits like time-saving and ease of use.
2. Added high-quality images, including lifestyle shots of the gadgets in action.

Results:

- Conversion rates increased by 35%.
- Average session duration improved by 40%.
- Customer feedback highlighted the improved product presentation.

Summary

Crafting effective product descriptions and images is essential for engaging customers, building trust, and driving sales.

Key Takeaways

1. **Descriptions:**
    - Focus on benefits, use conversational language, and structure content for readability.
    - Incorporate SEO techniques to improve discoverability.
2. **Images:**
    - Use high-quality visuals, showcase multiple angles, and include lifestyle or contextual shots.
    - Optimize image sizes for faster loading times and better performance.
3. **Alt Text:**
    - Ensure images are accessible and optimized for search engines with descriptive, keyword-rich alt text.

By combining compelling descriptions with visually appealing images, you can create a memorable shopping experience that encourages customers to click "Add to Cart." In the next chapter, we'll dive into designing high-converting product pages that integrate these elements seamlessly.

Chapter 11: Setting Up Payment Gateways: Secure and Seamless Transactions

One of the most critical components of any online store is its ability to securely and efficiently process payments. Payment gateways act as the bridge between your customers and the financial institutions that handle their transactions. Selecting the right payment gateway and configuring it properly in WooCommerce ensures your store can provide a seamless checkout experience while maintaining high security standards.

In this chapter, we will explore the importance of payment gateways, how to choose the right one for your business, and the step-by-step process for setting them up in WooCommerce.

What Are Payment Gateways?

Payment gateways are software applications that authorize and process transactions between your store and your customer's bank or credit card provider.

Key Functions

1. **Authorization:** Validates the customer's payment details and confirms sufficient funds or credit.
2. **Transaction Processing:** Transfers funds from the customer to your account.
3. **Encryption:** Ensures sensitive data, such as card numbers, is securely transmitted.

Examples of Popular Payment Gateways

- **PayPal**
- **Stripe**
- **Square**
- **Authorize.net**
- **Amazon Pay**

Factors to Consider When Choosing a Payment Gateway

1. Supported Regions

Some gateways operate globally, while others are region-specific. Verify that your chosen gateway supports the countries where you plan to sell.

2. Fees and Costs

- **Transaction Fees:** Charged per sale, typically as a percentage plus a flat fee.
- **Setup Fees:** Some gateways charge an initial setup cost.
- **Monthly Fees:** Certain gateways require a subscription.

- Compare these costs to ensure profitability.

3. Compatibility with WooCommerce

Most popular gateways have dedicated plugins for WooCommerce. Check if the gateway integrates seamlessly with your store.

4. Payment Methods

Choose a gateway that supports diverse payment options such as credit cards, debit cards, e-wallets, and alternative payments like cryptocurrency.

5. Security Features

Ensure the gateway is PCI DSS-compliant and offers fraud detection tools, encryption, and SSL support.

6. User Experience

A smooth, user-friendly checkout process reduces cart abandonment. Consider gateways that support:

- Saved payment details for returning customers.
- Local currency payments.

7. Customer Trust

Familiar gateways like PayPal and Stripe inspire trust and can boost conversions.

Step-by-Step Guide to Setting Up Payment Gateways in WooCommerce

Step 1: Install WooCommerce Payment Gateway Plugins

1. Navigate to your WordPress Dashboard.
2. Go to **Plugins > Add New.**
3. Search for your preferred payment gateway plugin (e.g., "WooCommerce Stripe Payment Gateway").
4. Click **Install Now**, then **Activate**.

Step 2: Access WooCommerce Payment Settings

1. In your WordPress Dashboard, go to **WooCommerce > Settings > Payments.**
2. You'll see a list of available payment gateways.

Step 3: Enable Your Chosen Gateway

1. Find your desired gateway from the list.
2. Click the toggle to enable it.
3. Click **Set Up** or **Manage** to configure the gateway.

Step 4: Configure Gateway Settings

Each gateway has unique settings. Below are general configurations:

1. **API Keys:** Obtain these from your gateway provider's dashboard and paste them into the corresponding fields.
2. **Transaction Mode:** Choose between live (real payments) and sandbox (testing environment).
3. **Currency Settings:** Ensure the gateway supports your store's default currency.
4. **Payment Methods:** Select which methods to offer (e.g., credit card, PayPal, Apple Pay).
5. **Checkout Display:** Customize how the gateway appears to customers at checkout.

Step 5: Test the Payment Gateway

1. Use sandbox mode to simulate transactions.
2. Verify the entire checkout process, including:
    - Adding items to the cart.
    - Entering payment details.
    - Completing the purchase.
3. Check if transactions appear correctly in your WooCommerce dashboard and gateway provider's account.

Step 6: Go Live

Once satisfied with testing, switch to live mode and start accepting real payments.

Popular WooCommerce Payment Gateways

1. PayPal

- **Advantages:**
    - Globally recognized and trusted.
    - Offers PayPal accounts and direct credit card payments.
- **Setup:** Easy integration with the WooCommerce PayPal Payments plugin.

2. Stripe

- **Advantages:**
    - Supports multiple currencies.
    - Allows recurring payments for subscriptions.
    - Offers fraud detection tools.
- **Setup:** Requires API keys from your Stripe account.

3. Square

- **Advantages:**
    - Great for omnichannel businesses with both physical and online stores.
    - Integrates inventory management.
- **Setup:** Use the WooCommerce Square plugin to connect your store.

4. Authorize.net

- **Advantages:**
    - Robust security features.
    - Supports a wide range of payment methods.
- **Setup:** Requires API login ID and transaction key from Authorize.net.

5. WooCommerce Payments

- **Advantages:**
    - Built specifically for WooCommerce.
    - Accepts major cards and Apple Pay.
- **Setup:** Available directly within WooCommerce settings.

Security Best Practices for Payment Gateways

1. SSL Certificate

Secure your site with an SSL certificate to encrypt data during transmission.

2. PCI DSS Compliance

Ensure your store meets Payment Card Industry Data Security Standards.

3. Regular Updates

Keep WordPress, WooCommerce, and payment gateway plugins updated to patch security vulnerabilities.

4. Fraud Prevention Tools

Enable fraud detection features like CVV verification and address matching.

5. Two-Factor Authentication (2FA)

Use 2FA for your payment gateway account to prevent unauthorized access.

Troubleshooting Common Payment Gateway Issues

1. Transactions Not Processing

- Check API key accuracy.

- Ensure your account is in live mode.

2. Gateway Not Showing at Checkout

- Verify the gateway is enabled in WooCommerce settings.
- Confirm the gateway supports your currency and region.

3. Customers Reporting Errors

- Test the checkout process in sandbox mode.
- Check server error logs for potential conflicts.

4. Payment Declined

- Verify the customer's details are correct.
- Contact your payment gateway provider for specific declines.

Enhancing the Checkout Experience

1. Minimize Friction

- Enable guest checkout to reduce barriers for first-time customers.
- Offer multiple payment methods to accommodate preferences.

2. Display Trust Signals

- Add security badges (e.g., "Secure Checkout") near the payment fields.

3. Streamline Mobile Payments

- Ensure your payment gateway supports mobile-friendly options like Apple Pay or Google Pay.

4. Send Confirmation Emails

- Provide instant order confirmation to reassure customers of successful payments.

Case Study: Boosting Conversions with Better Payment Options

Scenario:

A fashion retailer experienced high cart abandonment rates.

Identified Issues:

1. Limited payment options (only credit cards).
2. Confusing error messages at checkout.

Improvements Made:

1. Added PayPal and Stripe for broader payment options.

2. Simplified error messages with clear instructions.
3. Enhanced security by adding trust badges and enabling SSL.

Results:

- Cart abandonment rate dropped by 25%.
- Customer satisfaction scores improved significantly.

Summary

Setting up payment gateways in WooCommerce is a vital step in creating a secure and seamless shopping experience. By selecting the right gateway and configuring it properly, you ensure smooth transactions that build customer trust and drive sales.

Key Takeaways

1. **Gateway Selection:** Choose a gateway based on supported regions, costs, compatibility, and user experience.
2. **Setup Process:** Follow WooCommerce's step-by-step guide to integrate and configure your payment gateway.
3. **Security:** Protect customer data with SSL certificates, PCI DSS compliance, and fraud prevention tools.
4. **User Experience:** Offer diverse payment options, simplify the checkout process, and display trust signals.
5. **Testing:** Regularly test payment gateways to identify and resolve issues early.

With secure and efficient payment systems in place, your WooCommerce store is equipped to handle transactions confidently. In the next chapter, we'll discuss how to configure shipping options to ensure smooth product delivery.

Chapter 12: Configuring Shipping Options: Local, International, and Custom Rates

Shipping is a cornerstone of any e-commerce operation. Offering flexible, accurate, and cost-effective shipping options can enhance customer satisfaction, reduce cart abandonment, and boost repeat business. In WooCommerce, you have a powerful suite of tools to configure shipping for local, international, and custom needs, ensuring that your store caters to diverse markets efficiently.

In this chapter, we'll explore how to set up and optimize shipping options, covering everything from flat-rate shipping to advanced zone-based pricing and custom rates.

Understanding WooCommerce Shipping Options

WooCommerce provides a highly customizable shipping system divided into **shipping zones**, **methods**, and **classes**:

1. **Shipping Zones**
    - Define geographical regions where shipping rules apply.
    - Each zone can have multiple shipping methods.
    - Example: "Local Zone" for your city, "International Zone" for overseas shipping.
2. **Shipping Methods**
    - Determine how customers are charged for shipping in each zone.
    - Common methods: Flat Rate, Free Shipping, Local Pickup.
3. **Shipping Classes**
    - Categorize products with different shipping needs.
    - Example: Bulky items vs. standard parcels.

Step-by-Step Guide to Configuring Shipping in WooCommerce

Step 1: Enable and Access Shipping Settings

1. Go to **WooCommerce > Settings > Shipping** in your WordPress dashboard.
2. Ensure the **Shipping** tab is enabled.

Step 2: Create Shipping Zones

1. Navigate to **Shipping Zones** and click **Add Shipping Zone.**
2. Define the zone's name (e.g., "United States") and geographical region.
3. Add methods (Flat Rate, Free Shipping, etc.) to the zone.

Step 3: Add Shipping Methods

For each zone, click **Add Shipping Method** and select from:

- **Flat Rate:** Set a fixed shipping price.
- **Free Shipping:** Offer free delivery with or without conditions (e.g., minimum order amount).
- **Local Pickup:** Allow customers to collect orders from a designated location.

Step 4: Configure Each Shipping Method

1. Click **Edit** next to the method.
2. Define costs and conditions:
   - **Flat Rate:** Enter a fixed cost or use formulas for dynamic pricing (e.g., based on product weight).
   - **Free Shipping:** Set conditions like minimum spend or coupon usage.

Configuring Local Shipping Options

1. Local Zones

- Create a shipping zone for your city or region.
- Add Local Pickup or Flat Rate as methods.

2. Examples of Local Shipping Methods

- **Flat Rate for Local Delivery:** Charge $5 for orders within 20 miles.
- **Free Local Delivery:** Offer free shipping for orders above $50.
- **Local Pickup:** Provide an option for customers to pick up items from a physical store or warehouse.

3. Benefits of Optimized Local Shipping

- Reduced operational costs.
- Faster delivery times.
- Improved customer satisfaction through personalized service.

Setting Up International Shipping

1. Create an International Shipping Zone

- Define regions (e.g., Europe, Asia) or choose "Rest of the World" for global coverage.

2. Shipping Carriers for International Orders

Use reliable carriers like:

- DHL

- FedEx
- UPS
- USPS

3. Shipping Methods for International Zones

- **Flat Rate:** Charge a standard fee, e.g., $20 per international order.
- **Real-Time Rates:** Integrate plugins that fetch live carrier rates based on destination, weight, and dimensions.

4. Customs and Duties

- Inform customers about potential import duties.
- Use tools like **WooCommerce AvaTax** to calculate taxes automatically.

5. Offer Multiple Options

Provide a mix of affordable and express shipping. For example:

- **Standard International:** Delivery in 10–15 business days, lower cost.
- **Express International:** Delivery in 2–5 business days, higher cost.

Custom Shipping Rates and Rules

WooCommerce allows advanced customizations for unique business needs.

1. Shipping Classes

Categorize products into classes to create tiered rates.

- Example:
  - **Standard Products:** $10 flat rate.
  - **Bulky Products:** $25 flat rate.

How to Create Shipping Classes

1. Go to **WooCommerce > Settings > Shipping > Shipping Classes.**
2. Click **Add Shipping Class** and define:
   - Name (e.g., "Heavy Items").
   - Description (e.g., "Products weighing over 20kg").

Assigning Shipping Classes to Products

1. Edit a product in WooCommerce.
2. Under the **Shipping** section, select a shipping class.

2. Dynamic Pricing with Formulas

Flat Rate shipping supports formulas for complex pricing:

- **Base Fee + Per Product Fee:** $10 + ($2 * [qty])
- **Weight-Based Rates:** $5 + ($1 * [weight])

3. Use Plugins for Advanced Customization

- **Table Rate Shipping:** Define detailed shipping rules based on multiple factors like destination, cart total, and weight.
- **Conditional Shipping and Payments:** Set rules for specific shipping methods, such as restricting international shipping for certain products.

Tips for Streamlining Shipping Operations

1. Automate Processes

- Use plugins like **ShipStation** or **WooCommerce Shipping** to print labels and manage tracking.
- Sync your store with shipping carriers for real-time rate calculations and automatic updates.

2. Clearly Communicate Shipping Policies

- Display delivery times and costs on product pages and during checkout.
- Offer a dedicated shipping FAQ to address common concerns.

3. Provide Tracking Information

- Integrate tracking plugins so customers can monitor their orders.
- Examples: **AfterShip** or **WooCommerce Shipment Tracking.**

4. Offer Free Shipping Incentives

Encourage larger orders with free shipping thresholds. For example:

- "Free shipping on orders over $100."

5. Optimize Packaging

- Use lightweight, durable materials to reduce costs.
- Partner with eco-friendly suppliers for sustainable shipping options.

Case Study: Boosting Customer Satisfaction with Tailored Shipping

Scenario:

An online boutique faced complaints about high shipping costs and unclear delivery times.

Challenges:

1. Flat rates didn't reflect actual costs.
2. Lack of international options deterred global customers.

Solutions:

1. Integrated real-time carrier rates for accurate pricing.
2. Introduced tiered options: Free local delivery, standard, and express international shipping.
3. Added tracking features to enhance transparency.

Results:

- Customer satisfaction scores improved by 30%.
- International sales increased by 20%.

Common Challenges and How to Overcome Them

1. High Cart Abandonment Due to Shipping Costs

- Offer free shipping for orders above a certain amount.
- Display shipping costs early in the checkout process.

2. Delivery Delays

- Partner with reliable carriers.
- Communicate estimated delivery times clearly.

3. Complex International Regulations

- Use plugins to automate customs and tax calculations.
- Partner with carriers experienced in international logistics.

Summary

Shipping is more than a logistical necessity—it's a key factor in customer satisfaction and loyalty. WooCommerce provides a robust framework to configure shipping options for local, international, and custom needs, ensuring your store meets customer expectations efficiently.

Key Takeaways

1. **Shipping Zones:** Tailor shipping methods to specific regions for better service.
2. **Methods:** Use flat rates, free shipping, or carrier integrations based on your business model.
3. **Classes:** Categorize products for tiered rates and optimized shipping costs.
4. **Automation:** Streamline operations with plugins for labels, tracking, and rate calculations.
5. **Transparency:** Clearly communicate costs, delivery times, and tracking details to customers.

With a well-designed shipping system, your WooCommerce store is equipped to handle diverse customer needs while maximizing efficiency and profitability. In the next chapter, we'll delve into managing taxes and ensuring compliance with international tax regulations.

Chapter 13: Tax Settings Made Easy: Compliance Without Complexity

Taxes are an unavoidable part of running a business, especially in e-commerce, where sales often span multiple regions and jurisdictions. Navigating the complexities of tax compliance might seem daunting, but WooCommerce simplifies the process with robust tools for setting up, calculating, and managing taxes. By automating tax calculations and clearly displaying them to customers, you can ensure compliance while building trust and avoiding legal pitfalls.

In this chapter, we'll guide you through configuring WooCommerce tax settings, addressing common scenarios like VAT, GST, and sales tax, and integrating advanced tools for seamless compliance.

Why Tax Compliance Matters in E-Commerce

1. Legal Requirements

Failure to comply with tax laws can result in fines, penalties, and legal complications. Every region has unique tax obligations, and your store must adhere to them.

2. Customer Transparency

Displaying accurate taxes during checkout improves customer trust and reduces cart abandonment caused by unexpected costs.

3. Simplified Accounting

Correct tax settings make bookkeeping and filing tax returns straightforward, saving time and resources.

Overview of WooCommerce Tax Features

WooCommerce provides powerful features for tax management, including:

1. **Automated Tax Calculations**
   - Automatically calculates tax based on customer location.
   - Supports country-specific rules like VAT in Europe or GST in Australia.
2. **Configurable Tax Classes**
   - Apply different tax rates to different product categories (e.g., reduced rates for books).
3. **Customer Location-Based Taxation**
   - Taxes adjust dynamically based on customer shipping or billing addresses.
4. **Compatibility with Extensions**
   - Integrate tax automation tools like **Avalara AvaTax** or **TaxJar** for advanced functionality.

Step-by-Step Guide to WooCommerce Tax Settings

Step 1: Enable Taxes in WooCommerce

1. Navigate to **WooCommerce > Settings > General.**
2. Check the box for **Enable taxes.**
3. Save changes to activate the **Tax** tab in WooCommerce settings.

Step 2: Configure General Tax Settings

Go to **WooCommerce > Settings > Tax,** where you'll find the following options:

1. **Prices Entered With Tax:**
    - Choose whether product prices include or exclude tax.
    - Example: If you list a product as $10, does it include or exclude applicable taxes?
2. **Calculate Tax Based On:**
    - Customer billing address.
    - Customer shipping address.
    - Your store's base address.
3. **Shipping Tax Class:**
    - Apply a specific tax rate to shipping charges.
    - Optionally match the tax class to the products in the cart.

Step 3: Set Up Tax Classes

1. Tax classes allow different rates for various products.
    - Default classes: **Standard Rates, Reduced Rates, Zero Rates.**
2. Add custom classes if needed (e.g., "Luxury Items").

Adding and Editing Tax Rates

1. Define Standard Tax Rates

1. Navigate to the **Tax Rates** section under the **Tax** tab.
2. Click **Standard Rates** and fill in the following fields:
    - **Country Code:** Enter the two-letter country code (e.g., US, GB).
    - **State Code:** Specify the state, if applicable.
    - **ZIP/Postcode:** Define postal areas, or leave blank for entire regions.
    - **City:** Optionally narrow rates to specific cities.
    - **Rate %:** Enter the tax percentage (e.g., 10 for 10%).

- **Tax Name:** Give the rate a descriptive name (e.g., "Sales Tax").

2. Add Reduced and Zero Rates

1. Use the **Reduced Rates** and **Zero Rates** sections to configure:
    - Lower rates for specific products, such as groceries.
    - Zero tax for tax-exempt goods or services.

3. Apply Tax Classes to Products

1. Edit a product in WooCommerce.
2. Under the **Tax Class** field, select the applicable class (e.g., Standard, Reduced).

Handling Tax Scenarios

1. Value-Added Tax (VAT)

Common in Europe and other regions, VAT applies to most goods and services.

- **Configuring VAT in WooCommerce:**
    1. Enable taxes and add VAT rates under the **Standard Rates** section.
    2. Use extensions like **EU VAT Assistant** to handle cross-border rules, such as reverse charges.
- **Displaying VAT Inclusive Prices:**
    - Enable the option to display prices with VAT included.

2. Goods and Services Tax (GST)

Used in countries like Australia, GST is similar to VAT but has unique compliance requirements.

- **Setting Up GST:**
    1. Add GST rates under **Tax Rates.**
    2. Apply the tax class to applicable products.
- **GST Reporting:**
    - Use tools like **TaxJar** to generate GST-compliant reports for filing.

3. Sales Tax in the United States

Sales tax varies by state, city, and even ZIP code.

- **Configuring Sales Tax:**
    1. Add state-specific rates under **Tax Rates.**
    2. Integrate plugins like **WooCommerce Tax** or **Avalara AvaTax** for automatic calculations.

Automating Tax Calculations

1. Tax Automation Plugins

- **TaxJar:** Automates sales tax calculations and filings across the U.S.
- **Avalara AvaTax:** Real-time tax calculations based on customer location and product taxability.

2. Benefits of Automation

- Saves time and reduces errors.
- Ensures compliance with constantly changing tax laws.
- Simplifies tax filing with downloadable reports.

Best Practices for Tax Compliance

1. Keep Rates Updated

- Monitor changes in tax laws for regions where you sell.
- Use plugins or services that update rates automatically.

2. Provide Clear Tax Breakdown

- Display taxes as a separate line item in the cart and on invoices.

3. Maintain Accurate Records

- Store tax reports and receipts securely for audits.
- Use WooCommerce's reporting tools for summaries.

4. Know Your Exemptions

- Research tax exemptions applicable to your business or products.
- Configure tax settings to exclude exempt customers or goods.

5. Offer Tax-Inclusive Pricing Strategically

- For international customers, tax-inclusive pricing simplifies conversions.
- Test whether tax-inclusive or tax-exclusive pricing works better for your market.

Case Study: Streamlining Taxes for a Global Store

Scenario:

A store selling digital products globally struggled with VAT compliance in the EU and fluctuating sales tax rates in the U.S.

Challenges:

- Manually updating tax rates across regions.
- Confusion over VAT inclusion for digital products.

Solutions:

1. Integrated **TaxJar** for automated sales tax in the U.S.
2. Used **WooCommerce EU VAT Assistant** to calculate and collect VAT.
3. Configured separate tax classes for digital and physical products.

Results:

- Reduced manual effort by 80%.
- Ensured compliance with international laws, avoiding penalties.
- Improved customer trust with transparent tax displays.

Common Challenges and How to Solve Them

1. Overcharging or Undercharging Taxes

- Double-check tax settings and rates for each region.
- Use live rate plugins for accuracy.

2. Inconsistent Tax Displays

- Verify settings for displaying prices with or without taxes.
- Ensure consistency across product pages, carts, and invoices.

3. Managing Multi-Country Compliance

- Use automation tools to handle diverse tax laws.
- Hire a tax consultant if expanding to complex regions.

Summary

Tax compliance is a critical aspect of running an online store, but it doesn't have to be complicated. WooCommerce's tax settings, combined with automation plugins, provide an efficient way to manage taxes for local and international customers.

Key Takeaways

1. **Tax Settings:** Enable and configure taxes in WooCommerce to match your business needs.
2. **Classes and Rates:** Use tax classes to apply different rates to products.
3. **Automation:** Integrate tools like TaxJar and AvaTax for seamless calculations.

4. **Compliance:** Stay updated on tax laws and maintain accurate records.
5. **Transparency:** Display clear tax breakdowns to customers at checkout.

With these tools and best practices, you can simplify tax management, enhance customer trust, and focus on growing your e-commerce business. In the next chapter, we'll dive into managing shipping labels and tracking to ensure smooth order fulfillment.

Chapter 14: Managing Inventory: Stock Levels, Alerts, and Automation

Effective inventory management is critical to running a successful online store. Poor inventory practices can lead to stockouts, overstocking, or frustrated customers, ultimately affecting your profitability and reputation. WooCommerce offers robust inventory management tools to help you maintain optimal stock levels, receive timely alerts, and automate processes. This chapter will walk you through setting up and managing inventory for your online store, ensuring efficiency and customer satisfaction.

The Importance of Inventory Management

Before diving into the specifics of managing inventory in WooCommerce, let's explore why it's essential:

1. Preventing Stockouts and Overselling

Customers expect products to be in stock when they place orders. Running out of stock can lead to lost sales and customer dissatisfaction, while overselling creates logistical nightmares.

2. Cost Efficiency

Holding excess inventory ties up capital and increases storage costs. Optimized inventory levels reduce unnecessary expenses.

3. Enhancing Customer Satisfaction

Accurate inventory ensures customers can purchase without delays, improving trust and retention.

4. Simplifying Operations

Automation tools streamline inventory management, saving time and reducing human errors.

Getting Started with Inventory in WooCommerce

1. Activating Inventory Management

WooCommerce offers built-in tools for inventory tracking. To enable inventory management:

1. Go to **WooCommerce > Settings > Products > Inventory.**
2. Check the box for **Enable stock management.**
3. Configure general settings such as:
    - **Hold Stock:** Reserve stock for unpaid orders for a set time.
    - **Notifications:** Receive email alerts for low or out-of-stock items.
    - **Stock Display Format:** Choose how stock levels appear on product pages.

2. Assigning Inventory to Products

Inventory can be managed at the product level:

1. Edit a product in WooCommerce.

2. Under the **Inventory** tab:
    - **Manage Stock:** Check this box to enable stock tracking for the product.
    - **Stock Quantity:** Enter the current stock level.
    - **Allow Backorders:** Decide whether customers can order items that are out of stock.
    - **Low Stock Threshold:** Set the level at which you'll receive a low-stock alert.

Setting Up Inventory for Different Product Types

WooCommerce supports various product types, each requiring specific inventory settings.

1. Simple Products

For products without variations:

- Enter the stock quantity under the **Inventory** tab.
- Set low stock and out-of-stock thresholds.

2. Variable Products

For products with variations (e.g., sizes, colors):

1. Navigate to the **Variations** tab.
2. Manage stock for each variation separately:
    - Assign stock levels, low stock alerts, and backorder preferences for each option.

3. Digital Products

Since digital products don't require physical inventory, inventory tracking is usually disabled.

Managing Stock Levels

1. Real-Time Stock Updates

WooCommerce automatically adjusts stock levels as customers place orders. For example:

- A customer purchases 3 units of a product with 10 units in stock.
- The stock level updates to 7 units immediately.

2. Handling Stockouts

When stock reaches zero:

- WooCommerce marks the product as **Out of Stock.**
- If backorders are enabled, customers can continue purchasing.

3. Bulk Stock Management

For stores with large catalogs:

1. Use the **Product CSV Import Suite** to update stock levels in bulk.
2. Alternatively, adjust stock directly in the **Products** list view in the WordPress dashboard.

Using Alerts for Better Control

1. Low Stock Alerts

Low stock notifications ensure you restock products in time to avoid stockouts. Configure thresholds for:

- Individual products (in the **Inventory** tab).
- General settings under **WooCommerce** > **Settings** > **Products** > **Inventory.**

2. Out-of-Stock Notifications

Receive alerts when items are completely out of stock. This helps you quickly update your store or decide on replenishment strategies.

3. Customer Notifications

Consider using plugins to notify customers when out-of-stock items are back in stock. This can improve customer retention and sales.

Automating Inventory Management

1. Automation Plugins

WooCommerce supports several extensions to streamline inventory management:

- **ATUM Inventory Management:** Offers detailed stock reports and tracking.
- **Stock Sync for WooCommerce:** Syncs inventory across multiple channels and warehouses.
- **WooCommerce POS:** Ideal for syncing physical and online store stock levels.

2. Drop Shipping Integration

For drop shipping businesses, plugins like **AliDropship** automatically update inventory based on supplier availability.

3. Inventory Forecasting Tools

Use tools like **TradeGecko** to predict demand and optimize stock levels based on historical sales data.

Inventory Reporting in WooCommerce

WooCommerce includes built-in reporting features to help you monitor inventory.

1. Navigate to **WooCommerce > Reports > Stock.**

2. View detailed insights, such as:
    - Low stock items.
    - Out-of-stock products.
    - Most sold products.

Advanced Reporting Plugins

For more detailed analytics, consider plugins like:

- **Metorik:** Provides in-depth reports and inventory performance tracking.
- **Inventory Reports for WooCommerce:** Offers customizable stock reports.

Best Practices for Effective Inventory Management

1. Regular Stock Audits

Schedule periodic audits to reconcile physical stock with WooCommerce records.

2. Optimize Stock Levels

Avoid overstocking by analyzing historical sales trends and seasonal demand.

3. Set Accurate Reorder Points

Determine low stock thresholds that allow enough time for restocking.

4. Leverage Automation

Automate routine tasks like stock updates and alerts to save time and reduce errors.

5. Centralize Inventory Management

If you sell on multiple platforms (e.g., Amazon, eBay), use tools like **Sellbrite** or **ChannelAdvisor** to sync inventory across all channels.

Case Study: Streamlining Inventory for a Growing Store

Scenario:

A small fashion store expanded its catalog and struggled to manage stock levels across multiple variations, leading to frequent stockouts and overselling.

Challenges:

- Inconsistent stock updates.
- Lack of real-time alerts for low inventory.

Solutions:

1. Activated WooCommerce's stock management tools.

2. Integrated **ATUM Inventory Management** for detailed tracking.
3. Enabled low-stock alerts for individual products.

Results:

- Reduced stockouts by 70%.
- Improved operational efficiency with automated updates.
- Increased customer satisfaction through better stock availability.

Common Inventory Management Challenges

1. Overselling

- **Solution:** Enable stock management and prevent backorders for high-demand products.

2. Slow Moving Inventory

- **Solution:** Run promotions or bundle slow-moving items with popular products.

3. Demand Fluctuations

- **Solution:** Use inventory forecasting tools to predict sales trends.

4. Managing Returns

- **Solution:** Ensure returned items are quickly restocked to avoid discrepancies.

Summary

Efficient inventory management is a cornerstone of a successful e-commerce business. WooCommerce's built-in tools, combined with plugins and automation, empower you to maintain accurate stock levels, automate routine tasks, and provide a seamless shopping experience for customers.

Key Takeaways

1. **Stock Management:** Activate inventory tracking and configure product-level settings.
2. **Alerts:** Use low-stock and out-of-stock alerts to stay ahead of restocking needs.
3. **Automation:** Leverage plugins for syncing and automating inventory tasks.
4. **Reporting:** Regularly review inventory reports to identify trends and make informed decisions.
5. **Best Practices:** Optimize stock levels, schedule audits, and centralize management for efficiency.

By implementing these strategies, you'll reduce operational inefficiencies, enhance customer satisfaction, and ensure your store is always ready to meet demand. In the next chapter, we'll explore creating promotional strategies to boost your store's sales and customer engagement.

Chapter 15: Creating a User-Friendly Checkout Experience

The checkout process is the critical final step in an online shopping journey. It is where all of the efforts to attract, inform, and persuade a customer come together. A smooth and intuitive checkout process can significantly reduce cart abandonment rates and increase conversions, whereas a complicated or frustrating checkout experience can drive customers away, costing you sales.

This chapter will guide you through the process of creating a user-friendly, seamless checkout experience in WooCommerce. We'll explore best practices, customizable features, and strategies for making your checkout process both simple and secure while ensuring that customers complete their purchases with ease.

The Importance of a User-Friendly Checkout Experience

A well-designed checkout experience is crucial for many reasons:

1. **Reducing Cart Abandonment**: According to studies, cart abandonment rates are often high in e-commerce. Complicated checkout forms, unexpected shipping costs, or confusing payment options are among the top reasons customers leave without completing their purchases. A smooth checkout process minimizes these obstacles.
2. **Building Trust**: A streamlined and professional checkout can help instill trust. Security is a top concern for online shoppers, and displaying trust signals (such as SSL certificates) can reassure them that their sensitive data is safe.
3. **Enhancing User Experience (UX)**: A user-friendly checkout process reduces friction for customers, making them more likely to complete their purchase and return in the future.
4. **Increasing Conversion Rates**: A simplified and frictionless checkout leads to more completed transactions. The easier it is for customers to check out, the more likely they are to do so.

Key Elements of a User-Friendly Checkout Experience

A well-designed checkout process encompasses several key features:

1. Streamlined Checkout Process

One of the primary goals is to minimize the number of steps it takes for a customer to complete a purchase. WooCommerce offers a few options to reduce complexity:

- **Single Page Checkout**: Rather than forcing customers to go through multiple steps to complete their purchase, offer a single-page checkout where customers can fill in all necessary details on one page. This significantly reduces friction and improves conversion rates.
- **Guest Checkout**: Requiring customers to create an account can deter some from completing their purchase. Offering a guest checkout option allows customers to complete their purchase without the need to register. You can still encourage them to create an account after the purchase to improve future shopping experiences.

- **Auto-Fill Forms**: Use auto-fill functionality to help customers save time when entering their billing or shipping information. This is particularly helpful for returning customers or customers using Google Autofill.

2. Minimal Form Fields

Simplify the information required from customers. A complicated or lengthy form can turn people off, increasing the likelihood of abandonment. Keep the following tips in mind:

- **Limit the fields**: Only ask for the most essential information to complete the order. This typically includes the name, shipping address, phone number (optional), and payment details. Avoid unnecessary questions that do not directly contribute to the purchase.
- **Use proper field validation**: Make sure that customers can easily understand how to fill out form fields (e.g., "Please enter a valid email address"). Implement proper validation to minimize errors and frustration.

3. Clear Call-to-Action (CTA) Buttons

The "Checkout" or "Place Order" button should be clearly visible and easy to find. Use a contrasting color that stands out from the rest of the page. The language on the button should also be action-oriented and clear, such as "Complete Purchase" or "Place Order."

4. Real-Time Shipping Calculations

Customers expect transparency when it comes to shipping costs. Hidden shipping charges are a leading cause of cart abandonment. Provide real-time shipping calculations before the customer proceeds to the payment page. WooCommerce allows integration with various shipping carriers to automatically calculate shipping rates based on the customer's location.

- **Shipping Estimator**: Display a shipping calculator in the cart page or during checkout to let customers know how much they will pay for shipping.
- **Free Shipping Option**: If possible, offer a free shipping option and make it visible to customers (e.g., "Free shipping on orders over $50"). This can incentivize customers to add more products to their cart.

5. Display Order Summary and Breakdown

Providing customers with a clear and transparent order summary helps avoid confusion and ensures they know exactly what they are paying for. Include details such as:

- Itemized product prices
- Shipping costs
- Taxes
- Discount codes or coupons applied
- Total amount to be paid

This summary should be visible at all stages of the checkout process.

6. Mobile-Friendly Design

An increasing number of customers shop on mobile devices, making it critical to ensure that your checkout process is mobile-friendly. The layout, buttons, and forms should all be optimized for mobile screens. A responsive design adjusts automatically to any screen size, providing a smooth shopping experience.

Customizing the WooCommerce Checkout Process

WooCommerce offers a variety of settings and customization options that allow you to create a checkout process that works for your business. Here's how to customize WooCommerce to create the best possible experience for your customers:

1. Configure WooCommerce Checkout Settings

WooCommerce comes with a variety of checkout-related settings that you can adjust:

1. **Go to WooCommerce > Settings > Checkout**.
2. **Enable guest checkout**: This option allows customers to complete their purchase without creating an account.
3. **Choose payment gateways**: WooCommerce supports various payment methods, such as PayPal, Stripe, credit card, and more. Select the payment gateways you want to offer and configure them according to your preferences.
4. **Enable terms and conditions**: You can require customers to accept your terms and conditions before completing their purchase. This is especially useful if you're selling high-ticket items or require legal agreements.
5. **Enable shipping calculators**: Allow customers to estimate shipping costs based on their location before proceeding to the checkout page.

2. Install Checkout Plugins

WooCommerce's default checkout process can be further enhanced with plugins. There are many options available that can streamline and optimize the checkout process:

- **WooCommerce Checkout Field Editor**: This plugin allows you to add, edit, or remove fields from the checkout page. You can customize the form to ask only the necessary questions.
- **One Page Checkout**: This plugin allows customers to complete their entire order on a single page, reducing the number of steps and making the checkout process more efficient.
- **WooCommerce Direct Checkout**: This plugin simplifies the checkout process by skipping the cart page and sending customers directly to checkout.

3. Implement Trust Signals

Shoppers need to feel secure when making an online purchase. Implementing trust signals throughout the checkout process can help reassure customers and increase conversions:

- **SSL Certificate**: An SSL certificate secures your website and ensures that all data exchanged between the customer and your store is encrypted. Display the "https" and padlock symbol to reassure customers.
- **Trust Badges**: Show security badges like "Verified by Visa" or "PayPal Verified" near the payment section to instill confidence.
- **Money-Back Guarantee**: Offering a money-back guarantee can further reassure customers that they're making a safe purchase.

Testing and Optimization

Once you've set up your user-friendly checkout process, it's essential to test it to ensure it works as intended. Here are some tips for optimizing and testing your checkout experience:

- **A/B Testing**: Try different versions of your checkout page to see which one performs best. For example, test different CTA button colors or wording, or experiment with displaying shipping costs earlier in the process.
- **Customer Feedback**: Regularly gather feedback from customers about their checkout experience. You can use surveys or follow-up emails to ask for their input on what could be improved.
- **Performance Testing**: Make sure your checkout process is fast and responsive. Slow loading times can frustrate customers and lead to abandoned carts.

Summary

Creating a user-friendly checkout experience is essential for boosting conversions and improving customer satisfaction. By focusing on simplicity, transparency, and security, you can design a checkout process that guides customers smoothly through the final stages of their purchase.

Key Takeaways:

1. **Streamline the Process**: Minimize the number of steps and form fields required to complete a purchase.
2. **Provide Shipping Transparency**: Offer real-time shipping calculations and highlight free shipping options.
3. **Mobile Optimization**: Ensure your checkout process is fully responsive on mobile devices.
4. **Customize with Plugins**: Enhance the WooCommerce checkout process using plugins like Checkout Field Editor and Direct Checkout.
5. **Build Trust**: Use SSL certificates, trust badges, and clear money-back guarantees to build customer confidence.

A well-optimized checkout process will not only reduce cart abandonment rates but also encourage repeat customers, helping you to grow your online business successfully.

Chapter 16: Marketing Essentials: Coupons, Discounts, and Upselling

Effective marketing strategies are key to driving sales and growing your online store. In the world of e-commerce, offering coupons, discounts, and upselling opportunities are powerful tactics for attracting new customers, retaining existing ones, and boosting your revenue. These marketing techniques, when used strategically, can lead to increased conversion rates, improved customer loyalty, and a more profitable business overall.

In this chapter, we will explore how to leverage WooCommerce's built-in marketing tools—coupons, discounts, and upselling—while also introducing advanced strategies to elevate your marketing efforts.

The Power of Coupons and Discounts

Coupons and discounts are perhaps the most widely used e-commerce tools for driving sales. Whether you're offering a percentage-off, a fixed discount, or a free shipping deal, these incentives can create urgency, encourage larger purchases, and help you stand out in a competitive market.

1. Types of Coupons and Discounts

There are various types of coupons and discounts you can offer to your customers. Let's break down some of the most effective ones:

- **Percentage-Based Discounts**: A percentage discount is one of the most popular coupon types. For example, "Get 20% off your order." This type of coupon is effective because it provides clear value to the customer, and it scales with the purchase amount, making it ideal for higher-value items.
- **Fixed Amount Discounts**: Fixed amount discounts are ideal for smaller or fixed-price items. For example, offering "$5 off your next order" can help motivate customers to make a purchase, especially if they are on the fence.
- **Free Shipping**: Shipping costs are one of the top reasons customers abandon their carts. Offering free shipping on orders above a certain threshold (such as $50 or more) can encourage customers to buy more and increase average order value (AOV). Free shipping can also be used as a loyalty perk for returning customers.
- **Buy One Get One Free (BOGO)**: BOGO discounts are great for promoting clearance items or increasing order value. Offering a "Buy one, get one free" deal creates a sense of urgency and can help clear out inventory while attracting customers who love a deal.
- **Conditional Coupons**: Conditional coupons allow you to set specific requirements for the discount to apply. For example, you could offer "$10 off when you spend $50 or more" or "20% off on select items." These types of coupons encourage customers to spend more in order to qualify for the discount.

2. Creating and Managing Coupons in WooCommerce

WooCommerce makes it easy to create and manage coupons through the admin dashboard. To create a coupon:

1. Go to **WooCommerce > Coupons**.

2. Click **Add Coupon**.
3. Enter the **coupon code** (the code that the customer will enter during checkout).
4. Set the **discount type** (percentage or fixed amount) and the **coupon amount** (how much the discount will be).
5. Configure additional settings such as usage limits, expiration dates, and restrictions (e.g., minimum purchase amounts or product exclusions).

Once a coupon is created, you can view its performance through WooCommerce reports and adjust your marketing strategy accordingly.

3. Best Practices for Coupons and Discounts

While coupons and discounts are valuable marketing tools, it's important to use them wisely to avoid devaluing your brand or losing money. Here are a few best practices to follow:

- **Create urgency**: Use expiration dates or limited-time offers to encourage customers to act quickly. For instance, "Hurry, offer ends in 48 hours!"
- **Target specific customer segments**: Tailor your coupons to specific customer groups—new customers, repeat buyers, or those who have abandoned their carts. For example, offer a first-time purchase discount or a discount for those who haven't bought from your store in a while.
- **Set usage limits**: Limit how many times a coupon can be used to prevent abuse and ensure that your promotions remain profitable.
- **Monitor and optimize**: Track the performance of your coupons and adjust them based on what works. Are certain types of coupons driving more sales? Are certain discounts leading to increased cart abandonment? Use this data to refine your strategy.

The Art of Upselling and Cross-Selling

Upselling and cross-selling are two sales techniques that focus on increasing the value of a customer's order. While coupons and discounts encourage people to spend more, upselling and cross-selling directly involve recommending additional products or upgrades that complement the customer's purchase.

1. What is Upselling?

Upselling involves suggesting a higher-end or more expensive version of the product the customer is already interested in. The goal is to persuade the customer to purchase a more expensive product, resulting in a higher total sale.

For example, if a customer is looking at a basic laptop, you might suggest a more premium version with better specifications, highlighting the additional value it offers (e.g., faster processor, larger storage).

2. What is Cross-Selling?

Cross-selling, on the other hand, is the practice of suggesting complementary products that go well with the customer's current purchase. For example, if a customer is buying a smartphone, you might recommend a phone case, screen protector, or wireless earbuds. Cross-selling is a great way to increase your average order value (AOV) without the pressure of upselling.

3. Implementing Upselling and Cross-Selling in WooCommerce

WooCommerce provides built-in options for upselling and cross-selling. Here's how you can set them up:

- **Upselling**: To set up upselling, go to the **Product Edit page** in your WooCommerce admin dashboard. Under the "Linked Products" section, you can add "Upsells" by selecting other products that are more expensive or upgraded versions of the current item.
- **Cross-selling**: Cross-sells can be set up in a similar way. On the **Product Edit page**, in the "Linked Products" section, you'll find the option to add "Cross-sells." Select products that complement the item in the customer's cart (e.g., accessories, related products).

Once these products are linked, WooCommerce will automatically show upsell and cross-sell recommendations on the product and checkout pages.

4. Best Practices for Upselling and Cross-Selling

For upselling and cross-selling to be effective, you need to use these techniques strategically. Here are a few tips to maximize their impact:

- **Personalization**: Use customer data to suggest products that are tailored to the shopper's preferences. For example, suggest products based on their browsing history, past purchases, or items already in their cart.
- **Don't Overwhelm Customers**: Too many upsell or cross-sell suggestions can overwhelm and annoy customers. Limit the number of recommendations to two or three items.
- **Offer Value**: Make sure the upsell or cross-sell product adds value for the customer. For example, if you're upselling a product, focus on the additional benefits that justify the higher price.
- **Timing is Key**: Upsell offers are most effective when made at the right time. For instance, presenting an upsell after the customer has added an item to their cart but before they proceed to checkout works well. Cross-sells can be displayed during checkout, reminding customers of complementary items they may have missed.
- **Bundle Offers**: A great way to upsell or cross-sell is by offering bundle discounts. For instance, you could sell a product with a "Complete the Set" discount, encouraging customers to purchase a related product at a reduced price.

Advanced Marketing Techniques for Coupons, Discounts, and Upselling

While coupons and upselling are proven strategies, advanced techniques can make these marketing efforts even more powerful.

1. Dynamic Pricing and Discounts

Dynamic pricing is the practice of adjusting prices based on factors like demand, customer behavior, or competitor pricing. WooCommerce offers plugins that allow you to set up dynamic pricing rules based on customer group, product quantity, or seasonal trends.

2. Automated Follow-Up Emails and Cart Abandonment Reminders

Cart abandonment is a major issue for e-commerce stores. Many customers leave their carts without completing a purchase. To address this, you can set up automated email reminders to encourage customers to return to their carts and complete their purchase. Offering a small discount or free shipping in these emails can further incentivize them to finish the transaction.

3. Affiliate Marketing and Referral Programs

Encourage your existing customers to promote your store by implementing affiliate marketing or referral programs. With WooCommerce plugins, you can track referrals, offer commission to affiliates, and set up referral-based discounts for customers who bring in new business.

Summary

Coupons, discounts, and upselling are essential tools in your marketing arsenal, and WooCommerce makes it easy to implement them on your store. When used effectively, they can help increase conversions, improve customer loyalty, and boost average order values.

Key Takeaways:

1. **Coupons and Discounts**: Offering percentage discounts, fixed amount discounts, free shipping, and BOGO deals can drive sales, create urgency, and increase your average order value.
2. **Upselling and Cross-Selling**: Recommend higher-end products (upselling) or complementary products (cross-selling) to increase your revenue per customer.
3. **Best Practices**: Use targeted marketing, personalization, and A/B testing to ensure your promotional offers are effective and profitable.
4. **Advanced Techniques**: Implement dynamic pricing, cart abandonment email reminders, and affiliate/referral programs to further enhance your marketing strategy.

By mastering these techniques and integrating them into your WooCommerce store, you'll be well-equipped to grow your business, increase your customer base, and ultimately achieve greater success in online selling.

Chapter 17: Leveraging SEO for WooCommerce: Driving Organic Traffic to Your Store

Search engine optimization (SEO) is one of the most powerful tools at your disposal to drive organic traffic to your WooCommerce store. In today's digital landscape, consumers rely heavily on search engines like Google to discover products and make purchasing decisions. If your store isn't optimized for search engines, you risk losing potential customers to your competitors.

In this chapter, we'll dive into the world of SEO and explore how to leverage it for your WooCommerce store. We'll cover key strategies for optimizing your site's structure, products, and content to ensure you rank higher in search results and attract the right traffic to your store.

Why SEO is Crucial for WooCommerce Stores

Before we delve into specific techniques, let's understand why SEO is critical for WooCommerce stores. SEO is the process of optimizing your website so that it ranks higher on search engines. This includes both on-page and off-page optimization, such as improving content, keywords, site structure, and link building.

1. Free Traffic

The primary benefit of SEO is that it brings free organic traffic. When your store ranks high on search engines, it receives traffic without the need to pay for ads. Unlike paid advertising, which requires continuous investment, SEO offers long-term returns. A well-optimized store can bring in traffic month after month, as long as you maintain your SEO efforts.

2. Targeted Traffic

SEO helps you reach users who are actively searching for products similar to what you sell. By targeting the right keywords and optimizing your product pages, you can ensure that your store attracts users who are more likely to convert into paying customers.

3. Brand Authority and Trust

Websites that rank high in search results are often seen as more trustworthy and authoritative. Customers are more likely to trust your store if it appears on the first page of search results, which can help you build credibility in your niche.

4. Better User Experience

SEO is not just about optimizing for search engines; it's also about improving the user experience on your website. A well-structured, fast-loading site with quality content is not only more likely to rank higher, but it also provides a better experience for visitors, leading to higher conversion rates.

---

1. Keyword Research: The Foundation of SEO

Keyword research is the cornerstone of any SEO strategy. By identifying the right keywords, you can optimize your product pages, content, and meta tags to match the search intent of potential customers. Here's how to approach keyword research for your WooCommerce store:

1.1 Understanding Search Intent

Search intent refers to the reason behind a user's search. Are they looking to buy a product, learn more about a topic, or find a solution to a problem? Understanding search intent will help you target keywords that align with your customers' needs. There are three main types of search intent:

- **Navigational**: The user is looking for a specific website or brand.
- **Informational**: The user is looking for information about a product, service, or topic.
- **Transactional**: The user is ready to make a purchase or take action.

For WooCommerce stores, the focus should be on targeting **transactional** keywords. For example, if you sell eco-friendly shoes, keywords like "buy eco-friendly shoes online" or "best eco-friendly shoes for women" are likely to lead to conversions.

1.2 Using Keyword Tools

To find relevant keywords for your store, you can use tools like:

- **Google Keyword Planner**: A free tool that shows keyword volume, competition, and related terms.
- **Ahrefs**: A paid tool that provides detailed keyword research and competitive analysis.
- **SEMrush**: A comprehensive SEO tool with keyword research, backlink analysis, and competitor insights.
- **Ubersuggest**: A free tool by Neil Patel that offers keyword suggestions and SEO insights.

Make sure to focus on **long-tail keywords**, which are longer, more specific phrases. These are easier to rank for and are often more likely to convert. For instance, "best organic cotton t-shirts for men" is more specific and likely to attract customers ready to buy.

1.3 Analyzing Competitors

Look at the keywords your competitors are ranking for and identify gaps or opportunities. This will help you refine your keyword strategy and target terms that your competitors may have overlooked.

---

2. Optimizing Your Product Pages for SEO

Once you've identified your target keywords, the next step is to optimize your WooCommerce product pages. Each product page should be optimized to target relevant keywords while offering a seamless and engaging user experience.

2.1 Product Titles

Your product title is one of the most important on-page SEO elements. Make sure it includes your primary keyword and clearly describes the product. For example, instead of a generic title like "Shirt," use "Men's Organic Cotton T-Shirt – Eco-Friendly and Comfortable."

2.2 Product Descriptions

A well-crafted product description should provide detailed, valuable information about the product. Include your target keywords naturally within the text, but avoid keyword stuffing. Aim to answer any questions potential customers may have, such as the product's benefits, size guide, and material details.

Use bullet points to make the description easier to read and highlight important features like "eco-friendly materials" or "fits true to size."

2.3 High-Quality Images and Alt Text

Images are essential for e-commerce stores, as they help customers visualize products. However, images also play a role in SEO. When uploading product images, make sure to:

- **Optimize image sizes** for faster loading times.
- **Use descriptive file names** that include keywords (e.g., "organic-cotton-t-shirt-blue.jpg").
- **Add alt text** to each image. Alt text helps search engines understand what the image is about and can improve accessibility.

2.4 URL Structure

Ensure that your product page URLs are clean, short, and keyword-rich. For example, "yourstore.com/organic-cotton-t-shirt" is better than "yourstore.com/product/12345." This makes it easier for search engines and users to understand what the page is about.

2.5 Customer Reviews

Encourage customers to leave reviews for your products. Reviews not only help build trust with potential buyers but also provide fresh content for search engines to crawl. Make sure your product pages include a review section and consider offering incentives for customers to leave feedback.

---

3. Optimizing Your Store's Structure

A well-organized website structure helps search engines crawl your site more efficiently and makes it easier for users to navigate. The structure should be logical, intuitive, and simple to use.

3.1 Category and Product Organization

Organize your products into categories that make sense for your customers. For instance, a clothing store may have categories like "Men's Wear," "Women's Wear," and "Accessories." Each category page should also be optimized with relevant keywords.

3.2 Internal Linking

Internal linking helps search engines discover other pages on your site. Link to related products or categories within your product descriptions and blog posts to improve the visibility of other pages.

For example, if you're selling an eco-friendly t-shirt, link to related products such as eco-friendly jackets or pants.

3.3 Mobile Optimization

Mobile traffic accounts for a large percentage of e-commerce sales. Google also prioritizes mobile-friendly websites in its rankings. Ensure that your WooCommerce store is fully optimized for mobile devices by using a responsive theme, optimizing images for mobile, and testing the user experience on different screen sizes.

3.4 Site Speed

Site speed is a crucial factor for both SEO and user experience. Slow-loading websites can lead to higher bounce rates and lower search engine rankings. To improve your site speed, consider:

- **Optimizing images** and using image compression tools.
- **Using a content delivery network (CDN)** to speed up loading times.
- **Minimizing HTTP requests** by reducing the number of plugins and scripts on your site.

---

4. Off-Page SEO and Link Building

Off-page SEO refers to strategies that help improve your store's authority through external factors, primarily backlinks. Backlinks are links from other websites to your store, signaling to search engines that your site is trustworthy and valuable.

4.1 Building Backlinks

To improve your off-page SEO, you need to build high-quality backlinks. Some effective methods include:

- **Guest blogging**: Write valuable articles for other websites in your niche and include a link back to your store.
- **Influencer partnerships**: Partner with influencers or bloggers who can review your products and link back to your store.
- **Social media sharing**: Share your products on social media platforms and encourage others to share your content, which can indirectly help with link building.

4.2 Local SEO

If you have a physical store or are targeting customers in specific locations, local SEO is important. Optimize your Google My Business profile, create local content, and encourage local reviews to improve your visibility in local search results.

---

5. Measuring and Monitoring Your SEO Performance

SEO is an ongoing process, and it's essential to monitor your efforts and adjust your strategy based on performance. Use tools like Google Analytics and Google Search Console to track key metrics such as:

- **Organic traffic**: How many visitors are coming to your store from search engines?
- **Bounce rate**: Are users staying on your site, or are they leaving quickly?
- **Conversion rate**: Are your SEO efforts leading to sales?

By monitoring these metrics, you can refine your SEO strategy and continue to improve your WooCommerce store's performance.

Summary

SEO is a powerful tool for driving organic traffic to your WooCommerce store. By focusing on keyword research, optimizing your product pages, improving your store structure, building backlinks, and monitoring your performance, you can achieve higher search rankings and attract the right customers. The key to success with SEO is consistency and continuous optimization. As search algorithms evolve, so should your SEO strategy to stay ahead of the competition and achieve long-term growth for your WooCommerce store.

Chapter 18: Social Media Integration: Using Platforms to Boost Sales

In today's hyper-connected world, social media has become a powerful tool for businesses to reach, engage, and convert potential customers. For WooCommerce store owners, integrating social media into your marketing strategy can significantly boost visibility, drive traffic, and increase sales. Social media platforms are not just promotional tools—they are channels where customers interact with brands, discover products, and make purchasing decisions.

This chapter explores how to leverage social media to maximize your WooCommerce store's success, from choosing the right platforms to implementing specific strategies for engagement and sales.

Why Social Media Matters for E-Commerce

1. Expanding Your Reach

Social media platforms like Facebook, Instagram, TikTok, and Pinterest have billions of active users. By establishing a presence on these platforms, you can expose your brand to a global audience, attract new customers, and increase your store's visibility.

2. Building Trust and Community

Consumers trust recommendations from people they know or follow on social media. Engaging with your audience through comments, posts, and direct messages builds a sense of community and trust, which is essential for customer loyalty.

3. Driving Traffic to Your Store

Social media platforms are excellent for driving traffic to your WooCommerce store. With enticing visuals, compelling captions, and clickable links, you can direct users to your product pages and encourage purchases.

4. Leveraging Social Commerce

Social media platforms increasingly offer features that allow users to shop directly within the app. Features like Instagram Shopping and Facebook Shops make it easier for customers to browse and purchase your products seamlessly.

Choosing the Right Social Media Platforms

Not all social media platforms are created equal. To maximize your efforts, focus on the platforms that align with your target audience and product type.

1. Facebook

Facebook is a versatile platform suitable for almost every business. It offers robust advertising tools, a marketplace feature, and integration with WooCommerce through plugins like Facebook for WooCommerce.

2. Instagram

Instagram is highly visual, making it ideal for showcasing products with strong aesthetics, such as fashion, home decor, or food. Features like Instagram Stories, Reels, and Shopping allow businesses to connect with users in creative ways.

3. Pinterest

Pinterest is perfect for niche products, especially those related to fashion, home decor, recipes, or DIY projects. Many users turn to Pinterest for inspiration, making it a great platform for driving traffic to your store.

4. TikTok

TikTok's popularity has skyrocketed, especially among younger audiences. Its short-form video content is ideal for storytelling and product demonstrations. With TikTok Ads and the TikTok Shopping feature, it has become an effective platform for e-commerce.

5. LinkedIn

If your store targets professionals or sells B2B products, LinkedIn can be a valuable platform. Use it to network, share informative content, and promote your products to a professional audience.

6. YouTube

As the second-largest search engine, YouTube is a powerful platform for creating product tutorials, unboxings, and reviews. Videos can drive traffic to your store and improve your brand's credibility.

Integrating Social Media with WooCommerce

1. Social Media Plugins

WooCommerce offers various plugins to integrate social media platforms with your store. Some popular options include:

- **Facebook for WooCommerce**: Sync your WooCommerce products with your Facebook Shop and run targeted ads.
- **Instagram Feed Pro**: Display Instagram posts featuring your products directly on your website.
- **Pinterest for WooCommerce**: Integrate your product catalog with Pinterest to enable shopping pins.

2. Social Sharing Buttons

Add social sharing buttons to your product pages to encourage customers to share your products with their networks. Plugins like **AddThis** or **ShareThis** make this process simple.

3. Shoppable Posts

Platforms like Instagram and Facebook allow you to create shoppable posts, where users can view product details and click directly to purchase. To enable this, link your WooCommerce store to your social media accounts and tag products in your posts.

4. Live Shopping

Live shopping is an emerging trend where businesses showcase products in live streams, allowing users to purchase directly during the broadcast. Platforms like Instagram Live and Facebook Live support this feature.

Creating Engaging Social Media Content

To stand out on social media, your content must be engaging, authentic, and tailored to your audience. Here are some tips for creating content that resonates:

1. Visual Storytelling

High-quality visuals are essential for grabbing attention on social media. Invest in professional photography or use tools like Canva to create eye-catching graphics.

2. Behind-the-Scenes Content

Showcasing the process behind your products—whether it's designing, manufacturing, or packaging—adds a personal touch that resonates with customers.

3. User-Generated Content (UGC)

Encourage customers to share photos or reviews of your products and repost them on your social media. UGC builds trust and provides authentic proof of your product's quality.

4. Educational Content

Create content that educates your audience about your products or industry. For example, if you sell skincare products, share tips on creating a skincare routine or explain the benefits of specific ingredients.

5. Engaging Captions

Captions should be compelling and include a clear call to action (CTA). For example: "Shop now," "Click the link in bio," or "Tag a friend who would love this!"

Social Media Advertising for WooCommerce

While organic reach is valuable, social media advertising allows you to target specific audiences with precision. Platforms like Facebook, Instagram, and TikTok offer robust ad tools to promote your WooCommerce store.

1. Setting Up Ad Campaigns

Start by defining your campaign goal—whether it's brand awareness, traffic, or conversions. Use high-quality visuals and clear CTAs to maximize the impact of your ads.

2. Retargeting Ads

Retargeting ads remind users who have visited your store but didn't make a purchase. WooCommerce plugins like **Pixel Caffeine** make it easy to set up Facebook and Instagram retargeting campaigns.

3. Influencer Collaborations

Collaborate with influencers in your niche to promote your products. Influencers have loyal audiences who trust their recommendations, making this an effective way to drive sales.

Measuring Social Media Success

To ensure your social media efforts are paying off, track key performance metrics regularly. Use analytics tools like Facebook Insights, Instagram Analytics, or third-party tools like Hootsuite and Buffer.

1. Key Metrics to Monitor

- **Engagement Rate**: Likes, comments, shares, and clicks.
- **Traffic**: How much traffic social media is driving to your store.
- **Conversions**: The number of sales generated from social media efforts.
- **Reach and Impressions**: The number of people who saw your posts.

2. A/B Testing

Test different types of content, captions, or ads to see what resonates most with your audience. Use the results to refine your strategy.

Practical Tips for Success

- **Consistency is Key**: Post regularly to stay top of mind with your audience.
- **Engage Actively**: Respond to comments, messages, and mentions to build relationships with your customers.
- **Leverage Trends**: Stay updated on social media trends and adapt them to your strategy.
- **Collaborate**: Partner with other brands or influencers to expand your reach.

Summary

Social media integration is a vital component of a successful WooCommerce store. By choosing the right platforms, creating engaging content, leveraging advertising tools, and integrating social commerce features, you can drive traffic and boost sales. The key is to stay consistent, monitor performance, and adapt your strategy based on your audience's preferences. When done effectively, social media can transform your WooCommerce store into a thriving e-commerce business.

Chapter 19: Email Marketing for WooCommerce: Building Relationships with Customers

Email marketing remains one of the most effective tools for e-commerce businesses to connect with customers, foster loyalty, and drive sales. For WooCommerce store owners, email is not just a promotional tool; it's a way to build lasting relationships by providing value, addressing customer needs, and creating personalized experiences. This chapter delves into the strategies, tools, and best practices for leveraging email marketing to grow your WooCommerce business.

Why Email Marketing is Crucial for E-Commerce

1. Direct Communication

Email provides a direct line of communication with your customers, free from the limitations of social media algorithms. Your message lands straight in the customer's inbox, ensuring visibility.

2. High ROI

Email marketing offers a remarkable return on investment (ROI), with studies showing an average return of $36 for every $1 spent. Its cost-effectiveness makes it an essential component of your marketing strategy.

3. Personalization

Emails can be tailored to individual customers based on their behavior, preferences, and purchase history, creating a more engaging and relevant experience.

4. Retargeting and Retention

Emails are an excellent tool for retargeting customers who abandoned their carts, reminding them of your products, and encouraging them to complete their purchases. They also help maintain relationships with existing customers, fostering repeat business.

Essential Email Marketing Tools for WooCommerce

WooCommerce integrates seamlessly with several email marketing tools to help automate and optimize your campaigns. Here are some popular options:

1. Mailchimp for WooCommerce

This plugin allows you to sync your store with Mailchimp, enabling you to create automated campaigns, segment audiences, and track email performance.

2. Klaviyo

Klaviyo specializes in e-commerce email marketing, offering advanced segmentation and automation features. It integrates directly with WooCommerce to provide personalized customer experiences.

3. Omnisend

Omnisend is an all-in-one marketing automation tool that combines email with SMS, push notifications, and more. Its WooCommerce integration simplifies multi-channel marketing.

4. Sendinblue

Sendinblue is another excellent option, offering tools for email creation, automation, and analytics. It's user-friendly and ideal for beginners.

Building an Email List

Before you can send emails, you need a robust list of subscribers. Here are some strategies for growing your email list:

1. Opt-in Forms

Place opt-in forms on high-traffic areas of your website, such as the homepage, blog posts, and product pages. Tools like OptinMonster can help you create attractive, customizable forms.

2. Offer Incentives

Encourage visitors to subscribe by offering incentives such as discounts, free shipping, or exclusive access to content. For example, "Sign up now and get 10% off your first order!"

3. Exit-Intent Popups

Use exit-intent popups to capture leads from visitors who are about to leave your website. These popups can offer a last-minute incentive to join your email list.

4. Collect Emails During Checkout

Add a checkbox at checkout that allows customers to subscribe to your newsletter. Make sure it complies with GDPR and other data privacy laws.

5. Social Media Integration

Promote your email list on your social media platforms by highlighting the benefits of subscribing, such as receiving exclusive deals or being the first to know about new products.

Types of Emails for WooCommerce Stores

To maximize the effectiveness of your email marketing efforts, diversify the types of emails you send. Here are the key email types:

1. Welcome Emails

Welcome emails are the first impression of your brand for new subscribers. Use this opportunity to introduce your store, highlight your best products, and thank them for subscribing.

2. Product Promotions

Send promotional emails to showcase new arrivals, seasonal sales, or limited-time discounts. Use compelling visuals and clear CTAs to encourage purchases.

3. Cart Abandonment Emails

Cart abandonment emails remind customers of the items they left in their cart and nudge them to complete their purchase. Include an incentive like free shipping or a discount to sweeten the deal.

4. Order Confirmation and Shipping Updates

Transactional emails such as order confirmations and shipping updates keep customers informed and build trust. Add a personal touch to these emails to make them more engaging.

5. Post-Purchase Emails

Follow up with customers after a purchase to thank them, request reviews, or suggest complementary products. This helps maintain engagement and encourages repeat business.

6. Re-engagement Emails

Re-engagement emails target inactive subscribers with offers or updates to reignite their interest in your brand. For example, "We miss you! Here's 15% off your next purchase."

7. Newsletter Emails

Regular newsletters keep subscribers updated about your store, including new products, company news, or helpful blog posts. This fosters a long-term relationship with your audience.

Crafting Effective Emails

To ensure your emails are opened, read, and acted upon, follow these best practices:

1. Write Compelling Subject Lines

Your subject line is the first thing recipients see. Make it concise, intriguing, and relevant. For example, "Exclusive Offer Inside: 20% Off for 24 Hours!"

2. Personalize Your Emails

Use the recipient's name and tailor content based on their preferences or purchase history. Tools like Klaviyo and Mailchimp make personalization simple.

3. Keep It Mobile-Friendly

Most emails are opened on mobile devices. Use responsive email templates and concise content to ensure your emails look great on all screen sizes.

4. Include a Clear Call to Action (CTA)

Your CTA should guide the recipient to the next step, whether it's "Shop Now," "Learn More," or "Claim Your Discount." Make it prominent and easy to click.

5. Use High-Quality Visuals

Include eye-catching images and graphics to make your emails visually appealing. Show your products in action or use lifestyle imagery to connect with your audience.

6. Test and Optimize

A/B test different subject lines, layouts, or CTAs to see what resonates best with your audience. Use analytics to refine your strategy over time.

Automating Email Campaigns

Automation saves time and ensures timely, relevant communication with your customers. Here are some essential automated workflows:

1. Welcome Series

Create a sequence of emails to onboard new subscribers. Start with a warm welcome, then follow up with product highlights and incentives.

2. Cart Abandonment Series

Set up a series of cart abandonment emails to remind customers of their unpurchased items. Include incentives like discounts or free shipping in the second or third email.

3. Post-Purchase Follow-Ups

Automate thank-you emails, review requests, and recommendations for complementary products after a purchase.

4. Birthday or Anniversary Emails

Send personalized emails to celebrate your customers' birthdays or anniversaries with your store. Include a special discount or gift.

Measuring Email Marketing Success

Track these key performance metrics to evaluate your email marketing efforts:

1. Open Rate

The percentage of recipients who open your emails. Aim for an open rate of 15-25% or higher.

2. Click-Through Rate (CTR)

The percentage of recipients who click on links in your email. A CTR of 2-5% is typical for e-commerce campaigns.

3. Conversion Rate

The percentage of email recipients who complete a desired action, such as making a purchase.

4. Unsubscribe Rate

Monitor the percentage of subscribers who opt out of your emails. A rate above 0.5% may indicate a need to adjust your content or frequency.

5. Revenue

Track how much revenue your email campaigns generate. Tools like Mailchimp or Klaviyo can attribute sales directly to specific campaigns.

Summary

Email marketing is an indispensable tool for WooCommerce store owners, offering a direct, cost-effective way to engage customers, build relationships, and drive sales. By growing your email list, crafting personalized and visually appealing emails, automating workflows, and analyzing performance, you can create impactful campaigns that deliver results. When done right, email marketing not only boosts revenue but also strengthens customer loyalty, setting the foundation for long-term success in your e-commerce journey.

Chapter 20: Understanding WooCommerce Analytics: Metrics That Matter

Data is the backbone of informed decision-making in e-commerce, and WooCommerce analytics provides store owners with a wealth of information to optimize performance. By understanding the key metrics and learning how to interpret them, you can identify strengths, address weaknesses, and create strategies to maximize revenue. This chapter explores the essentials of WooCommerce analytics, including the most important metrics, tools for analysis, and actionable insights.

The Importance of Analytics in E-Commerce

1. Data-Driven Decision Making

Analytics eliminates guesswork. Instead of relying on intuition, you can base your decisions on concrete data, ensuring strategies are effective.

2. Identifying Trends

By analyzing customer behavior and sales trends, you can predict demand, prepare for seasonal shifts, and optimize inventory.

3. Measuring Success

Analytics enables you to track the performance of marketing campaigns, product launches, and other initiatives, helping you measure ROI and refine efforts.

4. Enhancing Customer Experience

Understanding your customers' preferences and behaviors allows you to tailor your offerings and improve user experience, leading to higher satisfaction and loyalty.

Key Metrics to Monitor in WooCommerce

1. Sales Performance Metrics

- **Total Sales**: Tracks overall revenue generated within a specific time frame.
- **Average Order Value (AOV)**: The average amount customers spend per transaction. Calculated as:

$$\text{AOV} = \frac{\text{Total Revenue}}{\text{Number of Orders}}$$

A higher AOV indicates more profitable sales.

- **Sales by Product**: Identifies top-performing products, helping you focus on popular items.

2. Customer Behavior Metrics

- **Customer Lifetime Value (CLV)**: The total revenue a customer is expected to generate during their relationship with your store.
- **Cart Abandonment Rate**: The percentage of customers who add items to their cart but do not complete the purchase. High rates often signal issues in the checkout process.

3. Traffic and Conversion Metrics

- **Conversion Rate**: The percentage of website visitors who make a purchase. Calculated as:

$$\text{Conversion Rate} = \left(\frac{\text{Orders}}{\text{Total Visitors}} \right) \times 100$$

- **Traffic Sources**: Identifies where your visitors come from, such as organic search, social media, or paid ads.
- **Bounce Rate**: The percentage of visitors who leave your site after viewing only one page. High bounce rates may indicate poor site design or irrelevant traffic.

4. Operational Metrics

- **Inventory Turnover Rate**: Measures how quickly your inventory is sold and replaced. A high turnover rate is generally positive, indicating strong sales.
- **Refund and Return Rates**: Tracks the percentage of orders that are refunded or returned. High rates may point to quality issues or mismatched customer expectations.

5. Marketing Metrics

- **Email Open and Click-Through Rates (CTR)**: Evaluates the effectiveness of your email campaigns.
- **Coupon Redemption Rate**: Measures how often customers use promotional codes, helping you gauge the success of discount strategies.

Built-In WooCommerce Analytics Tools

WooCommerce includes a robust analytics dashboard that simplifies data tracking. Key features include:

1. Overview Dashboard

This provides a snapshot of your store's performance, including sales, orders, and top-selling products. Customize the dashboard to focus on metrics most relevant to your business.

2. Reports

WooCommerce offers detailed reports in areas such as:

- **Revenue**: Track daily, weekly, or monthly revenue trends.

- **Orders**: Analyze order patterns and fulfillment statuses.
- **Stock**: Monitor inventory levels and identify low-stock items.

3. Segmentation

Segment your data by time period, product, or customer group for more precise analysis. For example, compare holiday sales to off-season performance.

4. Export Options

Export your data in CSV format for deeper analysis using tools like Excel or Google Sheets.

Advanced Analytics Tools for WooCommerce

For deeper insights, consider integrating third-party analytics tools:

1. Google Analytics

Google Analytics provides comprehensive data on website traffic, user behavior, and conversion paths. Use the WooCommerce Google Analytics Integration plugin for seamless setup.

2. MonsterInsights

MonsterInsights simplifies Google Analytics data, presenting it in an intuitive dashboard within your WordPress admin area.

3. Metorik

Metorik offers advanced reporting and segmentation features tailored specifically for WooCommerce. It includes real-time analytics and customer insights.

4. Kissmetrics

This tool focuses on customer behavior, helping you track individual user journeys and optimize your store for better conversions.

Interpreting WooCommerce Analytics

1. Identifying Strengths and Weaknesses

Use analytics to pinpoint what's working and what needs improvement. For example, if a product has a high bounce rate, consider improving its description or images.

2. Setting Benchmarks

Establish benchmarks for key metrics like conversion rate and AOV. Regularly compare your performance to these benchmarks to track progress.

3. Analyzing Customer Journeys

Map out customer journeys to identify friction points, such as a complicated checkout process or slow-loading pages.

4. Tracking Marketing Campaigns

Use UTM parameters in your marketing URLs to track the effectiveness of specific campaigns in driving traffic and sales.

Actionable Insights from Analytics

1. Optimizing Product Listings

- Highlight top-selling products prominently on your homepage.
- Use analytics to identify underperforming products and experiment with pricing or promotions.

2. Improving Conversion Rates

- Simplify navigation and reduce the steps in the checkout process.
- A/B test product pages to determine which elements drive conversions.

3. Enhancing Customer Retention

- Implement a loyalty program to reward repeat customers.
- Use email marketing to engage with customers who haven't purchased in a while.

4. Adjusting Marketing Strategies

- Focus on high-performing traffic sources while optimizing underperforming ones.
- Allocate more budget to successful ad campaigns.

Common Pitfalls in Using Analytics

1. Overlooking Actionable Data

Focusing on vanity metrics like total visitors without considering actionable insights can lead to missed opportunities.

2. Ignoring Data Quality

Ensure your analytics tools are set up correctly to avoid inaccurate or incomplete data.

3. Analysis Paralysis

Avoid getting overwhelmed by data. Focus on a few key metrics that align with your business goals.

4. Failing to Act

Analytics is only useful if it informs action. Regularly review your data and implement changes based on your findings.

Summary

WooCommerce analytics equips store owners with the tools to monitor performance, understand customer behavior, and optimize operations. By focusing on key metrics such as sales performance, conversion rates, and traffic sources, you can make data-driven decisions that improve your store's success. With built-in WooCommerce analytics and advanced tools like Google Analytics or Metorik, the ability to track and interpret data has never been more accessible. By leveraging these insights, you can refine your strategies, boost customer satisfaction, and drive sustainable growth for your online business.

Chapter 21: Scaling Your Store: Adding New Products and Features

Scaling your online store is a pivotal step in ensuring long-term success and staying competitive in the ever-evolving e-commerce landscape. As your business grows, expanding your product offerings and integrating new features can significantly enhance customer experience, drive sales, and increase revenue. This chapter delves into the strategies for adding new products, implementing advanced features, and managing the growth of your WooCommerce store effectively.

Understanding the Importance of Scaling

1. Meeting Customer Demands

As customer preferences and market trends change, scaling allows you to introduce products and features that align with their expectations.

2. Enhancing Revenue Streams

Adding diverse product categories and advanced functionalities opens new opportunities for revenue generation and cross-selling.

3. Staying Competitive

A growing catalog and innovative features help your store stand out in a crowded market, making it more appealing to both new and returning customers.

4. Future-Proofing Your Business

Scaling ensures your store remains adaptable and ready to handle increased traffic, sales volume, and customer interactions.

Expanding Your Product Catalog

1. Identifying New Product Opportunities

Adding new products starts with understanding your market and customer needs. Conduct research through:

- **Customer Feedback**: Analyze reviews and survey responses to identify gaps in your offerings.
- **Sales Data**: Use WooCommerce analytics to determine which categories are performing well and could benefit from additional products.
- **Competitor Analysis**: Study successful competitors for inspiration on trending or complementary items.

2. Diversifying Product Types

WooCommerce supports various product types that can enrich your store:

- **Physical Products**: Ideal for tangible goods such as clothing, electronics, or home decor.
- **Digital Products**: Perfect for downloadable content like eBooks, software, or courses.

- **Subscription Products**: Generate recurring revenue with memberships or subscription boxes.
- **Variable Products**: Offer options like sizes, colors, or bundles.
- **Services**: Add options for services such as consultations or custom orders.

3. Testing New Products

Before fully committing to a new product line, test its viability:

- **Limited Runs**: Introduce a small batch to gauge interest.
- **Pre-orders**: Allow customers to order ahead, validating demand before full production.
- **Crowdsourcing Ideas**: Engage your audience in product development through polls or surveys.

Streamlining Product Addition

Adding new products in WooCommerce involves these steps:

1. Creating Product Listings

- Navigate to **Products** > **Add New** in your WordPress dashboard.
- Enter essential details:
    - **Product Name**: Keep it clear and descriptive.
    - **Description**: Highlight key features and benefits.
    - **Price**: Set competitive pricing based on market research.
    - **Images**: Use high-quality visuals to attract attention.

2. Configuring Product Attributes

- Add attributes like size, color, or material under **Attributes**.
- Use these attributes to create variable products for more options.

3. Organizing Products

- Assign products to relevant categories and tags for better navigation.
- Utilize cross-selling and up-selling techniques by linking related products.

4. Optimizing for SEO

- Write keyword-rich titles, descriptions, and meta tags to improve visibility on search engines.
- Use WooCommerce SEO plugins like Yoast WooCommerce SEO for enhanced optimization.

Integrating Advanced Features

1. Implementing Product Filters

Product filters improve usability by allowing customers to sort products by:

- Price range
- Categories
- Attributes like size or color

Plugins like **Filter Everything** or **WooCommerce Product Filter** can streamline this process.

2. Enhancing Search Functionality

Install search enhancement plugins like **FiboSearch** to offer real-time results and better query handling, ensuring customers find what they're looking for quickly.

3. Adding Wishlists and Gift Registries

Wishlists encourage repeat visits and social sharing. Use plugins like **YITH WooCommerce Wishlist** to integrate this feature.

4. Introducing Product Personalization

Allow customers to customize products through features like:

- Text engraving
- Image uploads
- Custom dimensions

Plugins like **WooCommerce Product Add-Ons** make personalization seamless.

5. Supporting Multiple Languages and Currencies

For global expansion, integrate multilingual support using **WPML** and enable multi-currency functionality with plugins like **WooCommerce Multi-Currency**.

Managing Growth Efficiently

1. Scaling Infrastructure

As your store grows, ensure your hosting environment can handle increased traffic:

- Opt for **scalable hosting solutions** like SiteGround or Cloudways.
- Use a **Content Delivery Network (CDN)** to improve site speed globally.

2. Automating Processes

Reduce manual tasks to save time and improve accuracy:

- **Inventory Management**: Automate stock updates with plugins like **TradeGecko**.
- **Order Fulfillment**: Integrate fulfillment services like ShipStation for seamless shipping.
- **Email Marketing**: Automate follow-ups and promotional emails with tools like Mailchimp.

3. Leveraging Analytics for Continuous Improvement

- Regularly review WooCommerce analytics to monitor product performance and customer behavior.
- Use these insights to refine strategies and adjust offerings as needed.

4. Training Your Team

As your store scales, invest in training your staff to handle customer inquiries, manage inventory, and oversee marketing campaigns.

Scaling Challenges and Solutions

1. Maintaining Quality

Challenge: Rapid growth can compromise product or service quality. Solution: Partner with reliable suppliers and implement quality control processes.

2. Managing Costs

Challenge: Expansion often requires significant investment. Solution: Scale gradually, focusing on high-impact areas first to ensure sustainable growth.

3. Retaining Customer Experience

Challenge: Adding too many features or products can overwhelm customers. Solution: Prioritize intuitive design and usability when implementing changes.

Scaling Through Marketing Strategies

1. Cross-Selling and Upselling

Promote complementary products or higher-end alternatives on product pages and at checkout.

2. Expanding Marketing Channels

Reach new audiences by leveraging:

- Social media platforms like Instagram and Pinterest.
- Marketplace integrations such as Amazon or eBay.

3. Running Targeted Campaigns

Use customer data to create personalized marketing campaigns, such as product recommendations or exclusive offers.

Success Stories: Real-World Examples

- **Case Study 1**: A home decor store scaled by introducing customizable furniture options, leading to a 35% increase in sales within six months.
- **Case Study 2**: An online bookshop diversified into digital products, offering audiobooks and eBooks, which doubled their customer base.

Summary

Scaling your WooCommerce store is essential for sustained growth and long-term success. By strategically adding new products, optimizing existing offerings, and integrating advanced features, you can meet customer demands while enhancing revenue. Effective scaling involves leveraging analytics, automating processes, and maintaining high-quality standards to ensure customer satisfaction. With the right approach, you can transform your WooCommerce store into a thriving, scalable business that adapts seamlessly to the changing needs of the e-commerce landscape.

Chapter 22: Handling Customer Support: Tools and Best Practices

Exceptional customer support is a cornerstone of a successful e-commerce business. It builds trust, fosters loyalty, and drives repeat sales. For WooCommerce store owners, mastering customer support means utilizing the right tools and adopting best practices to ensure that every customer interaction is positive and efficient. In this chapter, we will explore the significance of excellent customer service, essential tools, and actionable strategies to enhance your support processes.

The Importance of Customer Support

1. Enhancing Customer Satisfaction

Prompt and effective customer support improves customer satisfaction, increasing the likelihood of repeat business and positive reviews.

2. Building Trust and Loyalty

Responding to inquiries and resolving issues quickly fosters trust. Loyal customers are more likely to advocate for your brand, contributing to organic growth.

3. Reducing Negative Feedback

Proactively addressing concerns can mitigate the risk of negative reviews and public complaints that could harm your brand's reputation.

4. Competitive Advantage

Superior customer support can set your store apart from competitors, creating a unique selling proposition in crowded markets.

Key Elements of Effective Customer Support

1. Accessibility

Make it easy for customers to contact you by providing multiple communication channels, such as email, live chat, phone, and social media.

2. Speed

Quick response times are critical in meeting customer expectations. Delays in resolving issues can lead to frustration and lost sales.

3. Personalization

Address customers by name and reference their order details to show you value their business and understand their concerns.

4. Proactivity

Anticipate potential issues and address them before customers reach out, such as sending updates about delays or stock availability.

5. Consistency

Ensure that all customer interactions align with your brand's tone, values, and policies.

Essential Tools for Customer Support in WooCommerce

1. Help Desk and Ticketing Systems

Help desk software organizes and tracks customer inquiries, ensuring no issue is overlooked. Popular options include:

- **Zendesk**: A robust ticketing system with automation and reporting features.
- **Freshdesk**: Offers multichannel support and integration with WooCommerce.
- **Awesome Support**: A WordPress plugin specifically designed for WooCommerce.

2. Live Chat Tools

Live chat allows for real-time assistance and is often preferred by customers. Consider tools such as:

- **Tawk.to**: A free live chat solution with customizable widgets.
- **LiveChat**: Provides advanced analytics and integration options.
- **Crisp**: Offers multichannel communication, including chat and email.

3. Email Management Tools

Centralize and manage support emails with tools like:

- **Gmail with Labels and Filters**: Simple yet effective for smaller businesses.
- **Zoho Desk**: An email ticketing tool with automation and reporting features.

4. Social Media Integration

Monitor and respond to customer inquiries on platforms like Facebook, Instagram, and Twitter using tools such as:

- **Hootsuite**: Streamlines social media messaging.
- **Buffer**: Manages and tracks engagement across platforms.

5. Knowledge Base and FAQs

Provide self-service options with a knowledge base plugin like:

- **Heroic KB**: Easy-to-use knowledge base plugin for WordPress.
- **Documentor**: Offers detailed FAQ and guide creation.

6. Chatbots and Automation

Automate routine responses and triage inquiries using AI-powered tools like:

- **ChatGPT-based bots**: Handle common questions and escalate complex issues.

- **ManyChat**: Ideal for Facebook Messenger automation.

Implementing Best Practices for Customer Support

1. Offer Multichannel Support

- Provide several communication options to cater to diverse customer preferences.
- Integrate tools to manage all channels from a single dashboard.

2. Train Your Team

Equip your support team with the skills and knowledge to handle various customer issues effectively. Training should cover:

- Product knowledge
- Communication skills
- Conflict resolution techniques

3. Set Clear Expectations

- Publish your response times for each channel. For example:
    - Emails: Within 24 hours
    - Live Chat: Immediate
    - Social Media: Within 1-2 hours
- Keep customers informed about the status of their inquiries.

4. Use Automation Wisely

Leverage automation for repetitive tasks, such as:

- Order status updates
- Shipping notifications
- FAQs responses via chatbots

5. Monitor and Improve Response Times

- Track response times using analytics tools.
- Identify bottlenecks and optimize workflows to reduce delays.

6. Collect Feedback

- Send follow-up emails or surveys after resolving issues to gauge customer satisfaction.
- Use feedback to identify areas for improvement.

Handling Common Customer Support Scenarios

1. Product Queries

- Provide detailed product descriptions and FAQs to minimize inquiries.
- Use live chat or a chatbot for quick answers to common questions.

2. Order Issues

- Have a clear process for handling order-related issues, such as delays or incorrect items.
- Communicate updates proactively.

3. Refunds and Returns

- Implement a transparent return policy and make it easily accessible on your website.
- Use tools like **Return Refund and Exchange for WooCommerce** to streamline the process.

4. Technical Problems

- Provide troubleshooting guides in your knowledge base.
- Work with your development team to address recurring technical issues.

5. Handling Difficult Customers

- Stay calm and empathetic, even in challenging situations.
- Offer solutions that align with your policies while prioritizing customer satisfaction.

Measuring the Effectiveness of Customer Support

1. Key Performance Indicators (KPIs)

Track metrics such as:

- **First Response Time (FRT)**: The time it takes to respond to a customer's initial inquiry.
- **Average Resolution Time (ART)**: The average time to resolve an issue.
- **Customer Satisfaction Score (CSAT)**: A survey-based metric measuring customer happiness.
- **Net Promoter Score (NPS)**: Gauges customer loyalty and willingness to recommend your brand.

2. Analyzing Support Tickets

- Identify patterns in customer inquiries to address recurring issues.
- Use insights to improve your processes or product offerings.

3. Monitoring Customer Feedback

- Regularly review reviews and ratings on your website and third-party platforms.
- Address negative feedback publicly and transparently.

Scaling Customer Support as You Grow

1. Hiring and Training Staff

- As your store grows, expand your support team to handle increased inquiries.
- Ensure all new hires receive comprehensive training.

2. Upgrading Tools

- Invest in enterprise-grade tools as your support needs evolve.
- Consider implementing a customer relationship management (CRM) system for enhanced efficiency.

3. Outsourcing Support

- For 24/7 coverage or multilingual support, consider outsourcing to a reputable support agency.

Summary

Providing excellent customer support is integral to building a successful WooCommerce store. By utilizing tools like help desks, live chat, and automation, you can streamline processes and improve efficiency. Best practices such as offering multichannel support, setting clear expectations, and training your team ensure every customer interaction is positive. Regularly monitoring KPIs and gathering feedback helps you identify areas for improvement and adapt as your store grows. With a proactive and customer-focused approach, you can turn support interactions into opportunities for building loyalty and driving long-term success.

Chapter 23: Mobile Optimization: Making Your Store Accessible Everywhere

In today's e-commerce landscape, mobile optimization is no longer optional—it's essential. With a significant portion of online shopping occurring on mobile devices, ensuring your WooCommerce store is mobile-friendly can mean the difference between growth and stagnation. Mobile optimization involves tailoring your store's design, functionality, and performance to provide a seamless shopping experience for users on smartphones and tablets. This chapter explores why mobile optimization is critical, how to achieve it, and the tools and techniques to make your store accessible everywhere.

Why Mobile Optimization Matters

1. The Rise of Mobile Shopping

- **Statistics Speak Volumes**: Over 50% of global web traffic comes from mobile devices. Mobile shopping, or m-commerce, has become a dominant force in retail.
- **User Expectations**: Customers demand a fast, intuitive, and visually appealing experience on mobile devices.

2. Enhanced User Experience

- A mobile-optimized store ensures visitors can navigate, browse, and purchase with ease, reducing frustration and bounce rates.

3. SEO Benefits

- Google uses mobile-first indexing, meaning it primarily evaluates the mobile version of your site for ranking. Poor mobile optimization can hurt your search engine visibility.

4. Increased Conversion Rates

- A streamlined mobile experience can significantly boost conversions by minimizing barriers in the purchasing process.

Key Elements of Mobile Optimization

1. Responsive Design

Responsive design ensures your website adapts to different screen sizes and resolutions. Benefits include:

- Improved usability across devices
- Consistent design and functionality
- Cost-effectiveness compared to maintaining separate desktop and mobile sites

2. Fast Loading Speeds

- Mobile users are less patient with slow-loading websites. Even a one-second delay can lead to a significant drop in conversions.

- Tools like **Google PageSpeed Insights** can help identify and fix performance bottlenecks.

3. Touch-Friendly Navigation

- Buttons, menus, and interactive elements should be large enough and spaced appropriately for easy tapping.
- Avoid requiring pinch-to-zoom gestures, as they can frustrate users.

4. Simplified Checkout Process

- Optimize your checkout for mobile by minimizing form fields, enabling guest checkout, and offering mobile payment options like Apple Pay and Google Pay.

Steps to Optimize Your WooCommerce Store for Mobile

1. Choose a Mobile-Friendly Theme

- Many WordPress themes are designed with mobile responsiveness in mind. Popular options include:
    - **Astra**
    - **OceanWP**
    - **GeneratePress**
- Test a theme's responsiveness before implementing it using tools like Google's Mobile-Friendly Test.

2. Optimize Images and Media

- Compress images using plugins like **Smush** or **ShortPixel** to reduce file sizes without compromising quality.
- Use responsive images that adjust to different screen sizes with the <srcset> attribute.

3. Enable Accelerated Mobile Pages (AMP)

- AMP provides a lightweight version of your store for faster loading on mobile devices.
- Use the **AMP for WP** plugin to implement AMP pages in your WooCommerce store.

4. Simplify Navigation

- Use a hamburger menu for compact navigation.
- Include a prominent search bar to help users find products quickly.

5. Test Across Devices

- Use testing tools like **BrowserStack** or **Responsinator** to preview your store on various devices and screen sizes.
- Regularly check for broken elements or formatting issues.

6. Leverage Mobile-Specific Features

- Enable push notifications for personalized offers.
- Incorporate location-based marketing for local promotions.

Optimizing Performance for Mobile

1. Use a Content Delivery Network (CDN)

A CDN speeds up content delivery by serving your store from servers closest to the user's location. Popular options include:

- Cloudflare
- BunnyCDN

2. Minimize HTTP Requests

- Combine CSS and JavaScript files where possible.
- Use lazy loading for images and videos to reduce initial page load times.

3. Optimize Your Hosting

- Choose a hosting provider optimized for WordPress and WooCommerce, such as SiteGround, Kinsta, or WP Engine.

4. Implement Caching

- Use caching plugins like **W3 Total Cache** or **WP Rocket** to store static versions of your site, reducing server load and speeding up page delivery.

Enhancing Mobile Usability

1. Focus on Readability

- Use legible fonts with adequate size (at least 16px for body text).
- Maintain high contrast between text and background for visibility.

2. Optimize Forms

- Limit required fields to essential information.
- Enable autofill options for faster input.

3. Streamline Product Pages

- Display key product information prominently.
- Use swipe gestures for image galleries.

4. Include Mobile Payment Options

- Simplify the checkout process by integrating mobile payment gateways like:
    - PayPal
    - Stripe
    - Apple Pay
    - Google Pay

Tracking Mobile Performance

1. Monitor Mobile Traffic

- Use **Google Analytics** to track the percentage of visitors accessing your store from mobile devices.
- Analyze metrics like bounce rates, session duration, and conversion rates for mobile users.

2. Gather Feedback

- Conduct surveys or usability testing with mobile users to identify pain points.
- Use heatmaps from tools like **Hotjar** to understand how mobile users interact with your store.

3. Regularly Update Your Store

- Keep plugins, themes, and WordPress core updated to ensure compatibility and security.
- Periodically audit your mobile experience to address new trends and technologies.

Mobile Optimization Tools and Plugins

1. Plugins

- **WPtouch**: Instantly creates a mobile-friendly version of your site.
- **Jetpack**: Offers responsive design features and performance enhancements.
- **Hummingbird**: Optimizes performance by reducing file sizes and enabling caching.

2. Testing Tools

- **Google Mobile-Friendly Test**: Checks if your store meets mobile usability standards.
- **Pingdom Tools**: Analyzes your site's loading speed and performance.
- **GTmetrix**: Provides detailed insights into performance issues.

3. Analytics and Feedback

- **Google Analytics**: Tracks user behavior and mobile performance metrics.
- **Hotjar**: Visualizes user interactions with heatmaps and session recordings.

Case Studies: Mobile Optimization Success Stories

Case Study 1: Local Boutique

A small boutique improved its mobile sales by 40% after simplifying its checkout process and implementing responsive images.

Case Study 2: Digital Product Store

A store selling eBooks saw a 25% increase in mobile conversions after integrating AMP and reducing page load times.

Challenges in Mobile Optimization

1. Balancing Features and Speed

- Challenge: Including too many features can slow down your site.
- Solution: Prioritize features that add value to the user experience and streamline others.

2. Keeping Up with Updates

- Challenge: New devices and screen sizes require constant adaptation.
- Solution: Regularly test and update your store to stay current.

3. Managing Costs

- Challenge: Optimizing for mobile can be resource-intensive.
- Solution: Start with high-impact improvements and scale efforts over time.

Summary

Mobile optimization is a crucial aspect of running a successful WooCommerce store. By implementing responsive design, optimizing for speed and usability, and leveraging mobile-specific features, you can cater to the growing audience of mobile shoppers. Tools like caching plugins, CDNs, and AMP can further enhance your store's performance on mobile devices. Regular testing and feedback collection ensure your store remains accessible and competitive. In a world where mobile commerce dominates, prioritizing mobile optimization will drive customer satisfaction, boost conversions, and set your store apart.

Chapter 24: WooCommerce Security: Protecting Your Store and Customers

E-commerce security is a critical component of running a successful WooCommerce store. Beyond protecting your business, it safeguards your customers' sensitive information, builds trust, and ensures compliance with regulations. Cyberattacks, data breaches, and malicious activities are constant threats, making it imperative to implement robust security measures. This chapter explores essential strategies, tools, and best practices to secure your WooCommerce store.

Why WooCommerce Security Matters

1. Protecting Customer Trust

- Customers entrust you with sensitive data, such as personal details and payment information.
- A single breach can damage your reputation and lead to customer loss.

2. Preventing Financial Loss

- Cyberattacks can result in monetary losses from fraud, ransomware, or lost sales due to downtime.

3. Compliance with Regulations

- Laws like GDPR, PCI DSS, and CCPA require strict data protection standards.
- Non-compliance can result in hefty fines and legal consequences.

4. Maintaining Business Continuity

- Unsecured websites risk downtime from attacks, disrupting operations and revenue flow.

Common WooCommerce Security Threats

1. Brute Force Attacks

- Hackers use automated tools to guess login credentials.

2. Malware Infections

- Malicious software can infect your store, steal data, or redirect customers to malicious sites.

3. Phishing Attacks

- Cybercriminals trick users into sharing sensitive information via fake emails or login pages.

4. SQL Injection

- Exploiting vulnerabilities to manipulate your database, compromising data integrity.

5. Denial-of-Service (DoS) Attacks

- Flooding your site with traffic to overwhelm servers and cause downtime.

WooCommerce Security Best Practices

1. Secure Your Hosting Environment

Choosing a reliable hosting provider is your first line of defense. Look for:

- **Firewall Protection**: Prevent unauthorized access to your server.
- **Regular Backups**: Ensure data can be restored in case of an attack.
- **SSL Certificates**: Encrypt data transfer between your site and users.

2. Keep Everything Updated

- Regularly update WordPress core, WooCommerce, themes, and plugins.
- Developers frequently patch vulnerabilities in updates.

3. Use Strong Passwords and Two-Factor Authentication (2FA)

- Require complex passwords for all users, including admins.
- Enable 2FA for an added layer of protection.

4. Limit Login Attempts

- Restrict failed login attempts to deter brute-force attacks.
- Use plugins like **Limit Login Attempts Reloaded**.

5. Regular Backups

- Schedule automatic backups using tools like **UpdraftPlus** or **BackupBuddy**.
- Store backups securely offsite or in the cloud.

Securing WooCommerce with Plugins

1. Wordfence Security

- Features include firewall protection, malware scanning, and login monitoring.
- Blocks malicious IPs automatically.

2. Sucuri Security

- Offers robust malware scanning and removal services.
- Monitors file integrity and protects against DoS attacks.

3. iThemes Security

- Helps fix common vulnerabilities and enforce strong password policies.
- Provides real-time updates on security breaches.

4. All-in-One WP Security & Firewall

- User-friendly tool for beginners.
- Offers file change detection, login lockdowns, and IP blacklisting.

Protecting Customer Data

1. Encrypt Data with SSL Certificates

- SSL certificates encrypt communication, protecting sensitive information.
- Most hosting providers offer free SSL through **Let's Encrypt**.

2. Secure Payment Gateways

- Use PCI-compliant payment gateways like PayPal, Stripe, or Authorize.net.
- Avoid storing sensitive payment information on your servers.

3. Mask User Data

- Limit the display of customer information in receipts, emails, and databases.

4. Implement Privacy Policies

- Clearly outline how customer data is collected, stored, and used.
- Ensure compliance with GDPR or other applicable laws.

Protecting the WooCommerce Admin Area

1. Change the Default Admin URL

- Default login URLs like yourdomain.com/wp-admin are easy targets.
- Use plugins like **WPS Hide Login** to change the login page URL.

2. Restrict Admin Access by IP

- Allow only trusted IP addresses to access the admin area.

3. Monitor User Activity

- Use activity logging plugins like **Activity Log** to track suspicious behavior.

4. Disable File Editing

- Prevent unauthorized changes to core files by disabling file editing in wp-config.php:

```
define('DISALLOW_FILE_EDIT', true);
```

Monitoring and Detecting Threats

1. Malware Scanning

- Regularly scan your site using plugins or online tools like **VirusTotal**.

2. Set Up Alerts

- Receive notifications for unauthorized login attempts or changes using plugins.

3. Perform Regular Security Audits

- Periodically review security settings and access permissions.

4. Use Security Headers

- Add security headers to your site to prevent common exploits:
  - **X-Content-Type-Options**: Prevents MIME-type sniffing.
  - **Content-Security-Policy**: Limits resources the browser can load.

Dealing with a Security Breach

1. Isolate the Problem

- Immediately take your site offline to prevent further damage.
- Identify the source of the breach using logs or monitoring tools.

2. Restore from Backup

- Replace the compromised site with a clean backup.

3. Remove Malware

- Use tools like **MalCare** or **Sucuri** to clean infected files.

4. Change All Passwords

- Update credentials for all user accounts and database access.

5. Notify Stakeholders

- Inform affected customers about the breach and steps being taken to address it.

Advanced Security Measures

1. Use a Web Application Firewall (WAF)

- Blocks malicious traffic before it reaches your site.
- Services like **Cloudflare** and **Astra Security** offer WAF solutions.

2. Database Security

- Use a strong database password.

- Change the default database prefix (wp_) to a unique one.

3. Disable Directory Listing

- Prevent hackers from viewing your file structure by disabling directory listing in .htaccess.

4. Secure FTP Access

- Use SFTP instead of FTP for secure file transfers.
- Restrict access to trusted IPs.

Case Studies: Security Success Stories

Case Study 1: Preventing Brute Force Attacks

A small e-commerce business reduced login attempts by 90% after implementing 2FA and limiting failed login attempts.

Case Study 2: Recovering from Malware

A WooCommerce store infected by malware used Sucuri's services to remove threats, implement a firewall, and prevent future breaches.

Challenges in WooCommerce Security

1. Balancing Security and Usability

- Excessive security measures can inconvenience users.
- Strike a balance by using intuitive tools like 2FA apps.

2. Staying Updated

- Security threats evolve constantly.
- Subscribe to security blogs or forums for updates.

3. Managing Costs

- Some advanced tools and services come with high fees.
- Focus on cost-effective solutions for critical areas first.

Summary

WooCommerce security is a multifaceted effort that requires vigilance and proactive measures. By securing your hosting environment, regularly updating software, encrypting customer data, and implementing security plugins, you can protect your store from common threats. Tools like SSL certificates, firewalls, and malware scanners provide additional layers of defense. Monitoring user activity and responding swiftly to breaches are critical to minimizing damage. Ultimately, prioritizing security builds customer trust, ensures compliance, and keeps your business running smoothly in an increasingly digital world.

Chapter 25: Troubleshooting Common WooCommerce Issues

Running a WooCommerce store is an exciting endeavor, but like any digital platform, it can sometimes encounter technical hiccups. Whether it's a plugin conflict, slow site performance, or checkout problems, troubleshooting these issues is crucial to maintaining a seamless shopping experience for your customers. This chapter will guide you through common WooCommerce issues, their causes, and step-by-step solutions, empowering you to manage your store with confidence.

Understanding the Nature of WooCommerce Issues

1. Common Categories of Issues

- **Compatibility Conflicts**: Problems often arise from incompatible plugins, themes, or outdated WooCommerce versions.
- **Configuration Errors**: Misconfigured settings can cause checkout errors or incorrect pricing.
- **Performance Bottlenecks**: Slow loading times and unresponsive pages can frustrate customers and hurt sales.
- **Payment Failures**: Errors in payment gateway integration can disrupt transactions.

2. Importance of Proactive Maintenance

- Regular updates, backups, and testing help prevent many issues before they impact your store.

Steps for Effective Troubleshooting

1. Identify the Problem

- **Observe Symptoms**: Note what isn't working—broken features, error messages, or slow performance.
- **Gather Feedback**: Check customer complaints or run tests to replicate the issue.

2. Isolate the Cause

- **Deactivate Plugins**: Temporarily disable plugins to see if the issue resolves.
- **Switch Themes**: Test using a default WordPress theme like Twenty Twenty-Three.
- **Review Logs**: Look at WooCommerce and server error logs for clues.

3. Test Solutions

- Implement changes incrementally, testing each one before moving to the next.
- Always back up your site before making significant modifications.

4. Document Resolutions

- Keep notes on issues and solutions for future reference or team training.

Troubleshooting Common WooCommerce Issues

1. Checkout Page Not Working

Symptoms: Customers can't complete purchases or are redirected to an error page.
Causes:

- Plugin conflicts or outdated WooCommerce.
- Incorrect page setup in WooCommerce settings.

Solutions:

1. **Verify Checkout Page Settings**:
   - Go to **WooCommerce > Settings > Advanced** and ensure the correct pages are linked under "Page setup."
2. **Test for Plugin Conflicts**:
   - Deactivate all plugins except WooCommerce, then reactivate one at a time to identify the culprit.
3. **Update WooCommerce**:
   - Ensure you're using the latest version of WooCommerce and WordPress.

---

2. Slow Website Performance

Symptoms: Pages take too long to load, especially during peak traffic.
Causes:

- Unoptimized images, excessive plugins, or server limitations.

Solutions:

1. **Optimize Images**:
   - Use tools like **Smush** or **Imagify** to compress images without losing quality.
2. **Use a Caching Plugin**:
   - Install plugins like **WP Rocket** or **W3 Total Cache** to reduce server load.
3. **Upgrade Hosting**:
   - Switch to WooCommerce-optimized hosting with better resources.
4. **Use a Content Delivery Network (CDN)**:
   - Implement CDNs like Cloudflare to serve content faster to global users.

---

3. Product Pages Not Displaying Properly

Symptoms: Missing product details, broken layouts, or images not loading.
Causes:

- Theme incompatibility or outdated templates.

Solutions:

1. **Check Theme Compatibility**:
    - Ensure your theme is WooCommerce-compatible.
2. **Update Template Files**:
    - Compare your theme's template files to WooCommerce's default templates and update as needed.
3. **Regenerate Thumbnails**:
    - Use the **Regenerate Thumbnails** plugin to fix image display issues.

---

4. Payment Gateway Issues

Symptoms: Transactions fail, or payment options don't appear at checkout.
Causes:

- Misconfigured settings, outdated gateway plugins, or server errors.

Solutions:

1. **Verify Gateway Configuration**:
    - Go to **WooCommerce > Settings > Payments** and ensure all settings are correct.
2. **Enable Debug Logging**:
    - Enable logging for the payment gateway to review detailed error messages.
3. **Update API Credentials**:
    - Ensure your payment gateway API keys are current and correctly entered.

---

5. Inventory Not Updating

Symptoms: Stock levels don't reflect recent purchases.
Causes:

- Database issues or caching problems.

Solutions:

1. **Check Inventory Settings**:

   - Go to **WooCommerce > Settings > Products > Inventory** and ensure inventory tracking is enabled.
2. **Clear Cache**:
   - Clear your site and server cache to update stock levels in real-time.
3. **Review Database Configuration**:
   - Ensure your database tables are optimized and free of errors.

---

6. Email Notifications Not Sending

Symptoms: Order confirmation emails are not delivered to customers or admins.
Causes:

- Misconfigured email settings or server issues.

Solutions:

1. **Check WooCommerce Email Settings**:
   - Go to **WooCommerce > Settings > Emails** and ensure notifications are enabled and email addresses are correct.
2. **Use an SMTP Plugin**:
   - Configure email delivery using plugins like **WP Mail SMTP** for reliable sending.
3. **Check Spam Filters**:
   - Ensure emails aren't being marked as spam by recipient servers.

---

7. Broken Links or 404 Errors

Symptoms: Links to products or pages result in 404 errors.
Causes:

- Permalink issues or deleted content.

Solutions:

1. **Reset Permalinks**:
   - Go to **Settings > Permalinks**, click "Save Changes" without modifying anything.
2. **Use a Redirection Plugin**:
   - Install a plugin like **Redirection** to manage broken links.
3. **Restore Missing Pages**:
   - Recreate or restore deleted content from backups.

---

8. Unexpected Errors After Updates

Symptoms: Features break or display errors following a plugin or theme update.
Causes:

- Incompatible updates or custom code conflicts.

Solutions:

1. **Test Updates on a Staging Site**:
    - Use a staging environment to test updates before applying them to your live site.
2. **Rollback Updates**:
    - Use plugins like **WP Rollback** to revert to a previous version.
3. **Consult Developer Documentation**:
    - Review release notes for changes that may affect your customizations.

Proactive Measures to Prevent Issues

1. Regular Backups

- Use tools like **UpdraftPlus** to schedule automatic backups.

2. Update Responsibly

- Keep WordPress, WooCommerce, themes, and plugins updated but always test changes.

3. Monitor Performance

- Use monitoring tools like **Google PageSpeed Insights** or **GTmetrix** to track and optimize site speed.

4. Use Reliable Plugins and Themes

- Only install plugins and themes from trusted developers with regular updates.

5. Maintain Logs

- Enable WooCommerce logs to track errors and activities for quick troubleshooting.

When to Seek Professional Help

If troubleshooting doesn't resolve the issue, consider:

- Reaching out to WooCommerce support.
- Hiring a certified WooCommerce developer for complex problems.
- Checking community forums or groups for advice.

Summary

Troubleshooting WooCommerce issues is an essential skill for every online store owner. By identifying problems, isolating causes, and implementing targeted solutions, you can quickly restore your store to full functionality. Regular maintenance, backups, and updates significantly reduce the likelihood of issues. When problems do arise, methodical troubleshooting ensures minimal disruption to your operations and customer experience. Adopting proactive measures and knowing when to seek expert assistance further strengthens your store's resilience in the dynamic world of e-commerce.

Chapter 26: Case Studies of Successful WooCommerce Stores

The flexibility and functionality of WooCommerce have made it the backbone of countless successful online stores worldwide. To illustrate its potential, this chapter delves into real-world examples of businesses that have leveraged WooCommerce to achieve remarkable success. Each case study highlights specific strategies, tools, and features used, offering insights to inspire your own e-commerce journey.

Case Study 1: The Artisan Boutique – Crafting a Unique Brand

Background:
The Artisan Boutique, a small business selling handmade pottery, faced challenges scaling beyond local craft fairs. The owners decided to create an online store to reach a global audience.

WooCommerce Strategy:

1. **Theme and Design**:
    - Selected a minimalistic and visually appealing theme to emphasize product photos.
    - Integrated a gallery page to showcase the artistic process, building trust with customers.
2. **Plugins Used**:
    - **Product Add-Ons**: Allowed customization options for engraving and designs.
    - **Mailchimp for WooCommerce**: Enhanced email marketing campaigns with personalized product recommendations.
3. **Marketing Techniques**:
    - Used social media integration to share behind-the-scenes content, increasing engagement.
    - Offered limited-time discounts and early access for email subscribers.

Results:

- Within six months, sales increased by 120%.
- Their unique products attracted international customers, with 40% of sales coming from repeat buyers.

Case Study 2: FitGear Pro – A Niche in Fitness Accessories

Background:
FitGear Pro specializes in high-quality resistance bands and fitness gear. Competing in a crowded market, the company needed a strategy to stand out.

WooCommerce Strategy:

1. **Targeted SEO**:
    - Focused on long-tail keywords like "best resistance bands for home workouts."

   - Published educational blog posts on fitness techniques, embedding product links.
2. **Performance Optimization**:
   - Implemented caching plugins and a CDN for fast page loads.
   - Ensured mobile optimization since 70% of their traffic came from smartphones.
3. **Customer Engagement**:
   - Used the **Points and Rewards** plugin to create a loyalty program.
   - Offered free digital workout guides with purchases, enhancing perceived value.

Results:

- Achieved a 300% increase in organic traffic within a year.
- The loyalty program boosted customer retention by 25%.

Case Study 3: LuxeHome Decor – Scaling to Enterprise Level

Background:
LuxeHome Decor started as a boutique furniture retailer but quickly outgrew its original platform due to scalability issues. Transitioning to WooCommerce provided the tools needed for enterprise-level growth.

WooCommerce Strategy:

1. **Advanced Inventory Management**:
   - Used plugins like **Stock Manager for WooCommerce** to track inventory across multiple warehouses.
   - Automated stock alerts to avoid overstocking or stockouts.
2. **Custom Features**:
   - Developed a custom quote request system for bulk orders.
   - Integrated augmented reality (AR) to let customers visualize furniture in their homes.
3. **International Expansion**:
   - Implemented a multi-currency plugin for seamless global transactions.
   - Adapted shipping options to cater to international customers.

Results:

- Sales increased by 450% over three years.
- International markets now account for 60% of revenue.

Case Study 4: FreshBite Organics – Delivering Farm-to-Table Products

Background:
FreshBite Organics delivers organic produce directly from farmers to customers. With a focus on freshness, they needed a WooCommerce store that could handle subscriptions and logistics efficiently.

WooCommerce Strategy:

1. **Subscription Model**:
   - Used the **WooCommerce Subscriptions** plugin to enable weekly and monthly produce boxes.
   - Allowed customers to customize their box contents based on preferences.
2. **Efficient Logistics**:
   - Integrated real-time shipping calculators to offer accurate delivery costs.
   - Used the **Delivery Slots** plugin to let customers choose convenient delivery times.
3. **Sustainability Messaging**:
   - Highlighted eco-friendly practices, such as using biodegradable packaging.
   - Partnered with local influencers to promote the brand.

Results:

- Subscriptions grew by 80% in the first year.
- Customer satisfaction ratings exceeded 95%, with many praising the delivery experience.

Case Study 5: TechGadget X – Thriving in a Competitive Market

Background:
TechGadget X, an online retailer for tech accessories, faced stiff competition from larger players. Leveraging WooCommerce, they built a niche following through innovation and excellent customer service.

WooCommerce Strategy:

1. **Personalized Shopping Experience**:
   - Used the **Product Recommendations** plugin to suggest items based on browsing history.
   - Created detailed product comparison charts for informed decisions.
2. **Enhanced Customer Support**:
   - Implemented a live chat feature using **Tawk.to** integration.
   - Offered extended warranties and easy returns to build trust.
3. **Seasonal Promotions**:
   - Ran flash sales during major shopping holidays.

- Used **Dynamic Pricing and Discounts** to create tiered discounts for bulk purchases.

Results:

- Monthly revenue doubled within a year.
- Their email list grew by 150%, driving repeat business through targeted campaigns.

Lessons from These Case Studies

1. **Know Your Audience**:
   - Tailor your store's design and features to your target customers. For example, Artisan Boutique emphasized storytelling, while TechGadget X focused on comparisons and live chat.
2. **Leverage Plugins Wisely**:
   - Plugins like Subscriptions, Product Add-Ons, and Points and Rewards can significantly enhance functionality and customer engagement.
3. **Focus on SEO and Marketing**:
   - FitGear Pro's success underscores the importance of SEO and educational content.
4. **Prioritize User Experience**:
   - Mobile optimization, fast loading times, and intuitive navigation are critical for conversion.
5. **Adapt to Scale**:
   - LuxeHome Decor demonstrates the value of scalable solutions like inventory management and AR integration.

Steps to Create Your Own WooCommerce Success Story

1. **Start with a Strong Foundation**:
   - Invest in quality hosting and a WooCommerce-compatible theme.
2. **Define Clear Goals**:
   - Whether it's expanding internationally or building a loyal customer base, align your strategy with your objectives.
3. **Regularly Analyze Performance**:
   - Use WooCommerce Analytics to identify strengths and areas for improvement.
4. **Engage with Your Community**:

    - Build trust through excellent customer service, transparent practices, and engaging content.

5. **Be Open to Innovation**:
    - Stay ahead by experimenting with new features and tools, as seen in the case of LuxeHome Decor's AR integration.

Summary

These case studies highlight how WooCommerce empowers businesses of all sizes to thrive in e-commerce. From niche artisans to enterprise-level retailers, the platform offers endless customization and scalability. Success hinges on understanding your audience, leveraging the right tools, and continuously optimizing your store. By learning from these examples and applying their strategies to your own store, you can pave the way for your WooCommerce success story.

Chapter 27: The Future of WooCommerce: Trends and Innovations

As e-commerce continues to evolve, WooCommerce remains at the forefront, offering adaptability and innovation to meet the ever-changing demands of online retail. This chapter explores the trends shaping the future of WooCommerce and the innovations that can help businesses thrive in a competitive marketplace.

---

1. The Rise of AI in WooCommerce

Artificial intelligence (AI) is revolutionizing the way e-commerce operates, and WooCommerce is no exception. AI tools are being integrated into WooCommerce to enhance personalization, streamline processes, and improve customer experience.

Applications of AI in WooCommerce:

- **Personalized Recommendations**: AI-driven plugins analyze customer behavior to suggest products tailored to individual preferences, increasing conversion rates.
- **Chatbots and Virtual Assistants**: Tools like ChatGPT for WooCommerce provide instant customer support, reducing response times and improving user satisfaction.
- **Dynamic Pricing**: AI tools can analyze market trends and competitor pricing to adjust product prices in real time, ensuring competitiveness.
- **Inventory Forecasting**: AI algorithms predict stock requirements based on sales trends, minimizing overstock and stockouts.

---

2. Headless Commerce: Decoupling Front-End and Back-End

Headless commerce is gaining traction as businesses seek faster, more flexible online stores. By decoupling the front-end (what customers see) from the back-end (where data is managed), WooCommerce users can create seamless shopping experiences across multiple platforms.

Benefits of Headless Commerce for WooCommerce:

- **Speed and Performance**: Front-end frameworks like React or Vue.js improve loading times, crucial for reducing bounce rates.
- **Omnichannel Integration**: Enables consistent experiences across websites, apps, and even IoT devices.
- **Customization**: Developers can build unique front-end experiences without being constrained by WordPress themes.

---

3. The Growth of Subscription-Based Models

Subscription e-commerce is booming, and WooCommerce is well-equipped to support this trend with plugins like **WooCommerce Subscriptions**. From meal kits to digital services, subscription models offer businesses a steady revenue stream while fostering customer loyalty.

Emerging Trends in Subscription Commerce:

- **Customization Options**: Customers expect personalized subscription plans tailored to their preferences.
- **Sustainability Focus**: Subscription boxes with eco-friendly themes are becoming increasingly popular.
- **Bundling Services**: Combining subscriptions with one-time purchases can increase average order value.

---

4. Embracing Sustainability in E-Commerce

As consumers become more environmentally conscious, WooCommerce stores are adopting sustainable practices to align with customer values. This trend not only appeals to eco-conscious shoppers but also strengthens brand identity.

Sustainability Features in WooCommerce:

- **Carbon Offset Plugins**: Tools like WooCommerce Carbon Checkout allow stores to offset the carbon footprint of their deliveries.
- **Sustainable Shipping Options**: Highlight eco-friendly shipping methods at checkout.
- **Transparency and Certifications**: Display certifications and detailed sourcing information to build trust with customers.

---

5. Voice Commerce: Shopping Through Smart Assistants

Voice commerce, driven by the rise of smart assistants like Alexa and Google Assistant, is changing the way people shop online. WooCommerce stores are beginning to adapt to this trend by integrating voice-enabled features.

Future Voice Commerce Features for WooCommerce:

- **Voice-Activated Search**: Enabling customers to find products using voice commands.
- **Voice Checkout**: Simplifying the checkout process for hands-free transactions.
- **Product Descriptions Optimized for Voice Search**: Using conversational keywords to rank higher in voice search queries.

---

6. The Power of Augmented Reality (AR) and Virtual Reality (VR)

AR and VR are reshaping the online shopping experience by allowing customers to interact with products in immersive ways. WooCommerce stores can leverage these technologies to stand out in competitive markets.

AR and VR Applications in WooCommerce:

- **Virtual Try-Ons**: Let customers try clothing or accessories virtually.
- **Interactive Product Previews**: Offer 3D models of products for customers to explore.
- **Virtual Showrooms**: Create an engaging shopping environment for customers browsing online.

---

7. Blockchain and Cryptocurrency Integration

Blockchain technology and cryptocurrencies are paving the way for secure and transparent e-commerce transactions. WooCommerce is embracing these innovations through plugins and integrations.

Benefits of Blockchain and Cryptocurrency in WooCommerce:

- **Enhanced Security**: Blockchain reduces the risk of fraud by offering immutable transaction records.
- **Global Reach**: Cryptocurrencies enable borderless payments without currency conversion fees.
- **Smart Contracts**: Automate order fulfillment and dispute resolution processes.

---

8. Data Privacy and Security Enhancements

With increasing concerns about data privacy, WooCommerce stores must prioritize secure customer data handling and compliance with global regulations.

Future Security Trends in WooCommerce:

- **Enhanced Encryption**: Protect sensitive customer information during transactions.
- **Compliance Tools**: Plugins to ensure GDPR, CCPA, and other regulatory compliance.
- **Biometric Authentication**: Introduce fingerprint or facial recognition for secure login and checkout.

---

9. Mobile-First Strategies

As mobile commerce continues to dominate, WooCommerce stores must optimize for mobile-first experiences. This trend involves designing for smaller screens without compromising functionality.

Key Mobile-First Features for WooCommerce:

- **Responsive Design**: Themes that adapt seamlessly to any device.
- **Progressive Web Apps (PWAs)**: Combine the best of web and app experiences.
- **One-Click Checkout**: Simplify the purchase process for mobile users.

---

10. Integration with AI-Powered Marketing Tools

The future of marketing for WooCommerce lies in automation and AI-driven tools. These innovations allow businesses to create highly targeted and effective campaigns.

AI Marketing Features:

- **Behavioral Email Campaigns**: Send automated emails based on user actions, like cart abandonment or repeat purchases.
- **Predictive Analytics**: Identify which products are likely to perform well based on past trends.
- **Social Media Ads Integration**: Sync WooCommerce products directly with platforms like Facebook and Instagram for dynamic ads.

---

11. Expansion of Marketplaces and Multivendor Stores

WooCommerce is evolving to support the growth of multivendor marketplaces, enabling businesses to host multiple sellers under one platform.

Future Multivendor Features:

- **Automated Vendor Management**: Streamline onboarding, payments, and commissions.
- **Customizable Vendor Dashboards**: Offer advanced analytics for individual sellers.
- **Marketplace-Specific SEO Tools**: Help vendors optimize their listings for better visibility.

---

12. The Role of 5G in E-Commerce

The rollout of 5G technology promises faster internet speeds and improved connectivity, unlocking new opportunities for WooCommerce stores.

5G's Impact on WooCommerce:

- **Enhanced Video Content**: Stream high-quality videos for product demonstrations without lag.
- **Improved Real-Time Features**: Support live shopping events and real-time customer interactions.
- **Better IoT Integration**: Enable smart devices to interact seamlessly with WooCommerce platforms.

Summary

The future of WooCommerce is brimming with opportunities, fueled by trends like AI, AR, sustainability, and blockchain. As technology advances, WooCommerce stores must adapt to changing consumer expectations and leverage innovative tools to stay competitive.

By embracing emerging technologies and aligning strategies with these trends, businesses can create cutting-edge WooCommerce stores that not only meet current demands but also prepare for the future.

The key lies in staying informed, experimenting with new features, and always putting the customer experience first.

Printed in Dunstable, United Kingdom

70707876R00080